First World War
and Army of Occupation
War Diary
France, Belgium and Germany

14 DIVISION
41 Infantry Brigade
York and Lancaster Regiment
18th (Service) Battalion
14 June 1918 - 31 May 1919

WO95/1896/2

The Naval & Military Press Ltd
www.nmarchive.com
Published in association with The National Archives

Published by

The Naval & Military Press Ltd

Unit 10 Ridgewood Industrial Park,

Uckfield, East Sussex,

TN22 5QE England

Tel: +44 (0) 1825 749494

www.naval-military-press.com

www.nmarchive.com

This diary has been reprinted in facsimile from the original. Any imperfections are inevitably reproduced and the quality may fall short of modern type and cartographic standards.

© **Crown Copyright**
Images reproduced by permission of The National Archives, London, England, 2015.

Contents

Document type	Place/Title	Date From	Date To
Heading	1896/2		
Heading	14th Division 41st Infy Bde 18th Bn York & Lancs Jun 1918- May 1919 From UK		
Heading	War Diary Of 18th York And Lancs Regt. From 14-6-18 To 30-6-18 May 19 Volume No. 1		
War Diary	Mayate	14/06/1918	18/06/1918
War Diary	Pirbright	19/06/1918	30/06/1918
Heading	War Diary Of 18th York And Lancs Regt From 1st July 1918 To 31st July 1918 Volume No 2		
War Diary	Brookwood	01/07/1918	03/07/1918
War Diary	Boulogne	04/07/1918	04/07/1918
War Diary	Hardinghen	05/07/1918	10/07/1918
War Diary	Herlinghem And Hocquinhem	11/07/1918	11/07/1918
War Diary	Tournehem	12/07/1918	12/07/1918
War Diary	Moulle	13/07/1918	31/07/1918
Operation(al) Order(s)	Operation Order No. 2 by Lt. Col. L.R. Jones M.C. Commanding. Warning Order. E	09/07/1918	09/07/1918
Operation(al) Order(s)	Operation Order No. 3 By Lieut. Colonel L.R. Jones M.C. Commanding 18th York & Lancs. Regt.	09/07/1918	09/07/1918
Operation(al) Order(s)	Operation Order No. 3/1 By Lieut. Colonel L.R. Jones M.C. Comdg. 18th. York & Lancs. Regt. Appendix 4	11/07/1918	11/07/1918
Operation(al) Order(s)	Operation Order No. 3/2 By Lieut. Colonel L.R. Jones M.C. Commanding 18th. York & Lancs. Regiment 18th. York & Lancs. Regiment Appendix 5	11/07/1918	11/07/1918
Operation(al) Order(s)	18th York & Lancs. Regt. Relief Order No. X By Lieut. Colonel L.R. Jones M.C. Commanding Appendix 6	16/07/1918	16/07/1918
Miscellaneous	18th Battn. York & Lancs. Regt. Addendum No. 2 To Battn. Order No. 1 Dated 27/6/18	01/07/1918	01/07/1918
Miscellaneous	18th Yorks. & Lancs. Regiment. Addendum No. 1 To Battn. Order No. 1 Dated 27.6.1918	30/06/1918	30/06/1918
Miscellaneous	Time Table	30/06/1918	30/06/1918
Operation(al) Order(s)	18th Bn. York & Lancs Amendment To Addendum No. 1 To Battalion Order No. 1 D/27-6-18	02/07/1918	02/07/1918
Operation(al) Order(s)	Battalion Order No. 1 By Lieut. Colonel L. R. Jones M.C. Commanding 18th. York & Lancs. Regt. Appendix I	27/06/1918	27/06/1918
Heading	War Diary Of 18th Battn York And Lancaster Regiment From 1st August 1918 To 31st August 1918 (Volume 3)		
War Diary	Moulle	01/08/1918	20/08/1918
War Diary	St Jan Ter Biezen	21/08/1918	28/08/1918
War Diary	Left Sub Sector	29/08/1918	31/08/1918
Operation(al) Order(s)	18th York & Lancaster Regiment Operation Order No. 4 By Lieut. Col. L.R. Jones, M.C. Commanding App 7	18/08/1918	18/08/1918
Miscellaneous	Table "A" to Accompany 18th York & Lancaster Operation Order No. 4		
Operation(al) Order(s)	18th York & Lancaster Regiment Operation Order No. 4/2 By Lieut. Col. L.R. Jones, M.C. Commanding	19/08/1918	19/08/1918
Operation(al) Order(s)	Appendix "A" To Operation Order No. 4/2 18th York & Lancaster Regiment	19/08/1918	19/08/1918

Type	Description	Start	End
Operation(al) Order(s)	18th York & Lancaster Regiment. Operation Order No. 5 By Lieut. Colonel L. Rodwell Jones M.C. Commanding. App 9	26/08/1918	26/08/1918
Operation(al) Order(s)	18th York & Lancaster Order No. 5/1 App 10	28/08/1918	28/08/1918
Heading	War Diary Of 18th York And Lancaster Regiment From 1st Sept 1918 To 30th Sept 1918 Volume 4		
War Diary	Ypres	01/09/1918	05/09/1918
War Diary	Siege Camp	06/09/1918	13/09/1918
War Diary	Ypres Sector	14/09/1918	19/09/1918
War Diary	St Laurent	20/09/1918	27/09/1918
War Diary	Reninghelst	28/09/1918	30/09/1918
Operation(al) Order(s)	18 Bn York & Lancs Regt. Order No 6 App I	04/09/1918	04/09/1918
Operation(al) Order(s)	18th Battn. York & Lancs. Regt. Order No. 7 App II	13/09/1918	13/09/1918
Operation(al) Order(s)	18th Batt. York And Lancs Regt. Order No. 8 App III	19/09/1918	19/09/1918
Heading	War Diary Of 18th York & Lancaster Regiment From 1st October 1918 To 31st October 1918 Volume 5		
War Diary	Ouderdom	01/10/1918	01/10/1918
War Diary	Messines	02/10/1918	05/10/1918
War Diary	Comines	06/10/1918	15/10/1918
War Diary	Messines	16/10/1918	17/10/1918
War Diary	Hazebrouck Factory	18/10/1918	18/10/1918
War Diary	Roncq	19/10/1918	20/10/1918
War Diary	Herseaux	21/10/1918	31/10/1918
Operation(al) Order(s)	18th Battalion York & Lancaster Regiment Order No 10 By Lieut Colonel C A Duncan Commanding App I	01/10/1918	01/10/1918
Operation(al) Order(s)	18th York & Lancaster Regt Order No 12 App II	06/10/1918	06/10/1918
Operation(al) Order(s)	18th York & Lancs. Order No 14 App 3	12/10/1918	12/10/1918
Operation(al) Order(s)	18th York & Lancaster Regt Order No 18 App 4	19/10/1918	19/10/1918
Operation(al) Order(s)	18th York & Lancaster Regiment Order No. 20 App 5	31/10/1918	31/10/1918
Heading	War Diary Of 18th York And Lancaster Regt. From 1/11/1918 To 30/11/1918 Volume 6		
War Diary	Espierres	01/11/1918	08/11/1918
War Diary	Wattrelos	09/11/1918	14/11/1918
War Diary	Bondues	15/11/1918	30/11/1918
Operation(al) Order(s)	Operation Orders No. 23 By Capt. C.W. Jefferson, Commanding, 18th Batt. York & Lancaster Regiment	08/11/1918	08/11/1918
Operation(al) Order(s)	Battalion Orders No. 24 By Capt. G.W. Jefferson, Commanding, 18th York & Lancaster Regt.	13/11/1918	13/11/1918
Heading	War Diary Of 18th York & Lancaster Regt. From 1st December, 1918 To 31st December, 1918 Volume VII		
War Diary	Bondues	01/12/1918	31/12/1918
Heading	War Diary Of 18th York And Lancaster Regt From 1/1/19 To 31/1/19 Volume 8		
War Diary	Bondues	01/01/1919	04/01/1919
War Diary	Tourcoing	05/01/1919	31/01/1919
Operation(al) Order(s)	18th York & Lancaster Regiment Order No. 22 App I	03/01/1919	03/01/1919
Heading	War Diary Of 18th York And Lancaster Regt. From 1/2/19 To 28/2/19 Volume 9		
War Diary	Tourcoing	01/02/1919	28/02/1919
Heading	War Diary Of 18th York And Lancaster Regt From 1/3/19 To 31/3/19 Volume 10		
War Diary	Tourcoing	01/03/1919	31/03/1919
Heading	War Diary Of 18th York And Lancaster Regt. From 1/4/19 To 30/4/1919 Volume 11		
War Diary	Tourcoing	01/04/1919	30/04/1919

Heading	War Diary Of 18th York And Lancaster Regt. From 1/5/1919 To 31/5/1919 Volume 12		
War Diary	Tourcoing	01/05/1919	31/05/1919

1981/2

14TH DIVISION
41ST INFY BDE

18TH BN YORK & LANCS
JUN 1918 - MAY 1919

From UK

WAR DIARY
— or —
INTELLIGENCE SUMMARY.

CONFIDENTIAL.

WAR DIARY

OF

18TH YORK AND LANCS. REGT.

VOLUME No. 1.

FROM 14-6-18.

May 19

ORIGINAL.

Army Form C. 2118.

WAR DIARY
INTELLIGENCE SUMMARY.
(Erase heading not required.)

Place	Date	Hour	Summary of Events and Information	Remarks and references to Appendices
Margate	14-6-18		The Battalion has been established with effect from 11th June 1918 under authority of War Office letter No. 20/Inf/1147 (A.G.2a) dated 1st June 1918 and is designated 18th YORK AND LANCASTER Regiment. Lt. Col. R.J. Andrew D.S.O. M.C. assumes command. Organising Battalion.	
do	15-6-18		do.	
do	16-6-18		do.	
do	17-6-18		Postings from other units to Companies as under:—	
			A Coy. From 18th Bn. York. Regt. 270 O.R.	
			" 24th " " " " 272 "	
			" 37th " Nads. Bur. 770 } 270	
			" 18th " York. Rgt. 100 }	
			B " " 27th " D.L.I. 220 } 250	
			C " " 26th " do 30 }	
			D " " Temporarily no return.	
			Officers as under are posted to Bn.:—	
			A/Lt. Col. T.M. Bullock Capt. J.S. Cogg. Capt. A.D. Rae.	
			Lt. A.D. Williams Lt. J. Kelly Lt. E.S. Sgt Badington	
			2/Lt. J. Green " A. Shipley w/c J. Thornton	
			" J.E. Falgarno " J. Tout " R. Thornton " E. Taylor	
			" J.G. Humpett " E. Saunders " R. Sumpton " E. Cohen	
				" A.C. Dickering

WAR DIARY or INTELLIGENCE SUMMARY

Army Form C. 2118.

Place	Date	Hour	Summary of Events and Information	Remarks and references to Appendices
Margate	18/6/18		Battalion left Margate for Stoney Castle Camp, Pirbright.	
Pirbright	19/6/18		Arriving Pirbright 11.15. Inspection of Training Staff of 29th Welsh. Battalion. Rifle inspection of 10 Officers and 47 O.R.'s made the Battalion Transit Officers. Lt. Jas. V.S. Hamilton M.C. 2/Lt. M. Burney Lt. Jas. to R. Jones M.C. 2/Lt. M. Gibson Capt. A.H. Pickering Capt. P. Raine M.C. Capt. T.R. Irvin M.C. Lord R. Nevill R.N.C. " Buchanan. " Neven	
do	20/6/18		Arriving Battalion and Kit Inspection.	
do	21/6/18		Arriving Companies. Specialist Training.	
do	22/6/18		Arriving Companies.	
do	23/6/18		Church Parade.	
do	24/6/18		Lewis Gun Rifle Firing on Bisley Ranges. Bombing Practice. Common Bombing Range. Two Instructors, Blackdown Barracks, Lt. Col. P.R. Jones M.C. took over command of the Battalion. Adjutants – Capt. Beckening, off West Yorks Rgt.	
do	25/6/18	10am	Commanding Officers Inspection of Coys. Dress, Full Marching Order.	
		3pm	Training under Coy arrangements. Two running Blackdown Bks.	

Army Form C. 2118.

WAR DIARY
INTELLIGENCE SUMMARY.
(Erase heading not required.)

Instructions regarding War Diaries and Intelligence
Summaries are contained in F. S. Regs., Part II.
and the Staff Manual respectively. Title pages
will be prepared in manuscript.

Place	Date	Hour	Summary of Events and Information	Remarks and references to Appendices
Rickarby C	26/9/18	9.30am	Rifle Firing on Century Butts and Lewis Gun Firing on Bog Siberia Range.	
do	27/9/18	9-4pm	Preparing Battalion for Overseas. Usu Arden drill, also drill & under Bg arrangements	
do	28/9/18	9-4pm	Preparing Battalion for Overseas. Close Arden drill, Specialist Training and Musketry	
do	29/9/18	9-4pm	Preparing Battalion for Overseas. Rifle and L.G. firing on Century Butts and Bg Siberia Ranges.	
do	30/9/18	9-4pm	Preparing Battalion for Overseas. Arm drill and Musketry. Specialist Training.	

Wilmot, LIEUT.-COLONEL,
COMMANDING 18th BN. YORK & LANCS REGT.

ORIGINAL. 14 D

Army Form C. 2118.

WAR DIARY

Vol 2

(Erase heading not required.)

Summary of Events and Information

CONFIDENTIAL.

WAR DIARY

OF

18TH YORK AND LANCS. REGT.

VOLUME No 2.

FROM 1st JULY 1918

TO 31st JULY 1918.

Place	Date	Hour		Remarks and references to Appendices

Army Form C. 2118.

WAR DIARY
or
INTELLIGENCE SUMMARY.
(Erase heading not required)

Instructions regarding War Diaries and Intelligence Summaries are contained in F.S. Regs., Part II and the Staff Manual respectively. Title pages will be prepared in manuscript.

Place	Date	Hour	Summary of Events and Information	Remarks and references to Appendices
Brookwood	1.7.18		Preparing for overseas. All companies on the range	
do	2.7.18		do. Class III now dispatched to Rifles. All companies bath	
do	3.7.18		Battalion entrained for France. Arrived Southampton. Bn. entrained Southampton camp.	Appendix 1
			Line operation order No. 1. Appendix I attached and marked	
Boulogne	4.7.18		2nd Battalion (North. Div. 9.35) for Havinghen arrived 2 p.m. Bn. billeted for inspection	
Havinghen	5.7.18		Bn. training	
do	6.7.18		Inspected by Ford Milner, Secy of State for War. Bn. specialist training	
do	7.7.18		Church Parade	
do	8.7.18		Inspected by Asst Inspector of Drafts. Specialist training	
do	9.7.18		Bn. specialist training. Warning order, to be prepared to move to Sperleque area. Received operation order No. 2	
do	10.7.18		Bn. moved to Herlingham and Hoquinghen. Operation order No. 3 Appendix No. 3 attached and marked. Bn. to report Bn. billeted	Appendix 3
Herlingham and Hoquinghen	11.7.18		Now complete 12 noon. Bn. billeted. Operation order No. 3/1 Appendix No. 4 attached and marked. Bn. move to Tournehem. Now complete 12 noon.	Appendix 4
Tournehem	12.7.18		Bn. move to Moulle. Operation order No. 3/2. Appendix No. 5 attached and marked now complete 12.30 p.m. Bn. billeted	Appendix 5
Moulle	13.7.18		Bn. training. Inspection of Lewis Guns by C.O.	
	14.7.18		Church Parade	
	15.7.18		Field General Court martial on Pte. Hoges No. 6,604. Pte. E. Saunders. Bn. specialist training	
	16.7.18		All companies on the range. Army Promulgation of Field General Court martial	
	17.7.18		Brigade inspected by G.O.C. Ind. Army. Promulgation of Field General Court martial No. 6,604. Pte. Saunders. E. Bn. training	
	18.7.18		Bn. specialist training	
	19.7.18		Medical Inspection by Asst. Inspector of Drafts	
	20.7.18		(a) Boys on the range. A-B Coys Company training	
	21.7.18		Church Parade. Kit and Billet Inspection	

WAR DIARY
or
INTELLIGENCE SUMMARY.
(Erase heading not required.)

Army Form C. 2118.

Instructions regarding War Diaries and Intelligence Summaries are contained in F.S. Regs., Part II. and the Staff Manual respectively. Title pages will be prepared in manuscript.

Place	Date	Hour	Summary of Events and Information	Remarks and references to Appendices
Houlle.	22.7.18		Lecture by Divl. Gas Officer to all Officers. Bn. training on Bn. area. Lewis Gun firing.	App.
	23.7.18		Bn. training. C.O. held conference with all O.C.'s & O/c's to discuss with reference to training.	App.
	24.7.18	6 am, 6.30am	Platoon Competitions in rapid fire. Night Brigade Outpost Scheme	App. App.
	25.7.18		Platoon Inspections, Drill, Gas Training, Musketry Tests.	App.
	26.7.18		"A" and "B" Gas Drill and Section Drill. "A" and "B" Companies in the attack.	App.
			"C" and "D" Companies Range Firing - Rifle and Lewis Gun.	
	27.7.18		"C" and "D" Companies Outposts. "A" and "B" Companies Lewis Gun and Rifle Sections firing on "D" Range, Musketry, Bombing and Specialist training.	App.
			2/Lt. H. White joined Unit 27/7/18	
	28.7.18		Church Parades. 2/Lt. J.E.H. Humfrey died natural causes in Hospital	App.
	29.7.18		Companies in attack, Outposts, Specialist Training	App.
	30.7.18		Firing on Range. Rifle and Lewis Gun.	App.
	31.7.18		Musketry, Bombing, Platoon Drill and Specialist Training. Battalion scheme as per attached order marked company in attack	Cct. App. 6.

app......

[signature]
COMMANDING 13th Bn. DCLI

APPENDIX 2

SECRET.   Copy No...13..

OPERATION ORDER No. 2 by
LT. COL. L.R. JONES M.C. COMMANDING.   573/14

WARNING ORDER.   9.7.18.

Ref. Maps - CALAIS & HAZEBROUCK.

    41st. Infantry Brigade Group will proceed by march route from HARDINGHEM area to EPERLECQUES Area on 10th. July, probably staging night 10/11th. July in the RECQUES Area.

                                                                   [signature]

Issued at 5 pm.   Capt. & Adjt.

DISTRIBUTION.

1. C.O.   9. Quartermaster.
2. 2nd. in Command.   10. Transport Officer.
3. Adjutant.   11. Medical Officer.
4. O/C A. Coy.   12. R.S.M.
5. O/C B. Coy.   13. Bde. H.Q.
6. O/C C. Coy.   14 & 15 War Diary
7. O/C D. Coy.   16 & 17 File.
8. H.Q. Coy.

SECRET. Appendix no 3   OPERATION ORDERS No. 3.   Copy No....1....
                     BY LIEUT. COLONEL L.R. JONES M.C. COMMANDING
                                  13th. York & Lancs. Regt.
Ref. Maps.   CALAIS & HAZEBROUCK.   9.7.18.

1.   14th. Division, less Divisional Artillery and R.Es will move by march route from HARDINGHEM AREA to EPERLECQUES AREA commencing on July 10th. The move will be carried out by short daily stages.

2.   41st. Infantry Brigade Group consisting of the following units will move on July 10th. to LICQUES AREA in accordance with attached march table (not attached):-
           41st. Infantry Brigade.

3.   On arrival in the LICQUES AREA the Battalion will be located as under:-
           13th Y & L   HARBINGHEM & HOCQUINGHEN.

4.(a) All troops will march for 20 minutes and halt for 10 minutes in every half hour. Halts to take place at 10 minutes to and 20 mins. past the clock hour.
 (b) 200 yds interval will be maintained between Companies and between Companies and First Line Transport.
       Not less than half a mile will be maintained between Battalions Field Ambs, Train Coy. and S.A.A. Section.
 (c) No smoking except during halts.
 (d) Any man falling out must be in possession of a chit signed by an officer.
 (e) O/C D. Coy will detail a party of 1 Officer and 10 O.R. to march in rear of the Battalion to collect stragglers.

5.   O/C Companies and Headqrs. will render a Falling Out State as soon as possible after arrival in billets.

6.   41st. Infantry Brigade Group will continue to march on 11th. July; destination will be notified later.

7.   Supply arrangements for the move will be as laid down in Bde. Office No. Q/19/57 dated 9.7.18.
       Baggage Wagons will report to the Battalion to-night 9th. July.

8.   One Lorry will be provided for the Battalion. This lorry will be at 41st. Inf. Bde. H.Q. at 8a.m. 10.7.18 & guides will be arranged to meet this lorry at the above time and place.

9.   Practice S.A.A., Targtes etc. will be taken to the new area under arrangements to be made by the Quartermaster.
       All Tents and Stores drawn from the Area Commandant will be handed in to the Transport Lines by 6.45 a.m. 10.7.18. The Transport Officer will be responsible that these are handed into the Area Commandant before the Battalion leaves and receipts obtained for same, and handed to the Adjutant on arrival at the new area.

10.   O/C Companies (including H.Q) will detail a rear party of 1 N.C.O. and 6 men to clean up Billets Latrines etc. A representative from the Area Commandant will be at Company H.Q. at 8 a.m. A

Continued overleaf.

Sheet 2

will be obtained from this representative that Billets, Latrines etc. have been left in a clean and sanitary condition. This certificate will be handed in to the Orderly Room on arrival in new Billets.

11. **Parades.** Parades will be as follows:—

    A. Coy. in road outside their billets at 9 a.m.
    'B' & 'C' Coys. in road by Transport Lines at 9 a.m.
    D. Coy. Road junction quarter-mile N. of V. in HERONVAL 9 a.m.
    Transport 9 a.m. in its own lines.
    Bn. H.Q. outside Orderly Room at 8.40 a.m.
    Companies and Transport will parade ready to march off by the above times. Cookers will accompany companies.
    Dress - Full Marching Order.
    Order of March - A, B, C, D, H.Q, Transport.

12. **Officers' Valises.** Officers' Valises and Mess Stores will be stacked outside their prespective company H.Q. by 7.30 a.m. 10.7.18

13. **Route.**
    Starting Point - Quarter-mile N. of V. in HERONVAL at 9 a.m. -
BOURSIN - SANGHEM - HERBINGHEM.

14.   REVEILLE   6 a.m.
    BREAKFAST 7 a.m.

15. ACKNOWLEDGE.

                                                    Captain & Adjutant.
                                                    18th York & Lancaster Regt.

Issued at 11.30 pm

DISTRIBUTION.
1. C.O.   9. Quartermaster.
2. 2/i/c.   10. Transport Officer.
3. Adjutant.   11. Medical Officer.
4. O/C A. Coy. 12. R.S.M.
5. O/C B. Coy. 13. Bde. H.Q.
6. O/C C. Coy. 14 & 15 War Diary
7. O/C D. Coy. 16 & 17 Files.
8. O/C Hdqrs.

SECRET   Appendix 4   Copy No. 6

OPERATION ORDER No. 3/1 BY
LIEUT. COLONEL L. R. JONES M.C. COMDG.
18th. York & Lancs. Regt.

Ref. Maps - CALAIS & HAZEBROUCK.   11.7.18.

1. In continuation of Battalion Order No. 3, the Battalion will continue to march to the EPERLECQUES AREA to-day 11.7.18.

2. The instructions contained in para. 4 of the above order will be complied with. O/C B. Coy. will detail a party of 1 Officer and 10 Other Ranks to march in rear of the Battalion to collect stragglers.
   (a). All transport personnel will wear Full Marching Order (Drivers will not wear packs). One Cook will march behind each cooker. The remaining personnel attached to the Transport will march as a formed party in rear of the Transport.

3. O/C Companies will render a Falling Out State as soon as possible after arrival in Billets.

4. Supply arrangements will be as follows:-
   11th. July - Refilling will take place at TOURNEHEM Church at 7 p.m. for consumption 13th.
   12th. July - Refilling will take place at MOULLE Church at 7 p.m. for consumption 14th.
   Supply Wagons will draw and deliver to units on both dates.

5. Railhead from 13th. July will be at WATTEN.

6. S.A.A. Section, D.A.C. will detail 5 G.S. Wagons to report to each Battalion on receipt of this order. These wagons will remain with the Battalions until arrival in the EPERLECQUES AREA when they will rejoin the S.A.A. Section.
   No Lorries are available.

7. 44th. Field Ambulance will arrange to collect Sick from units present locations one hour after departure.

8. O/C Companies (including Bn. H.Q.) will detail a rear party of 1 N.C.O. and 6 men to clean up billets, latrines etc. These parties will be collected and marched to destination by an Officer to be detailed by O/C B. Cpy.

9. Parade. Parades will be as follows:-
   A. Coy. On road outside billets 7 a.m.
   B. Coy. at 3 cross roads 100 yds. below Bn. Orderly Room 7 a.m.
   Hdqrs.   do   do   do
   D & C Coys. on Road outside Billets 7.30 a.m.
   Transport on road adjoining Transport Lines 7.30 a.m.
   Transport and Companies will be ready to march off at the above times.
   Dress - Full Marching Order. Order of march D - C - A - B - H.Q. - Transport.
   Cookers will accompany Companies.

'Continued overleaf'.

SECRET

OPERATION ORDER No. 3. BY
LIEUT.COLONEL L. P. JONES M.C. COMG.

Ref. Maps - CALAIS & HAZEBROUCK 1/100,000.

1. In continuation of Operation Order No. 2 the Bn. will continue to march to

   (a). All transport personnel will wear Full Marching Order Drivers.

   Other Ranks to march in rear and will not wear packs. The contents of the packs will be placed in the valises. A joined party in charge of an N.C.O. will march in rear as escort.

2. O/C companies will render a Rolling Off State as soon after arrival in Billets.

3.

4. 11th. July. A meeting will take place at TOURNEHEM Church at 7 p.m. for consideration.
   13th. " A meeting will take place at MOULLE Church at 7 p.m. for consideration.

   Bns. to draw and deliver to units on both dates.

   Railhead from 13th. July will be at WATTEN.

6. S.A.A. Section, D.A.C. will detail 2 G.S.Wagons to report to each Battn. and will detail in the MERCK-ST-LIEVIN area when they will rejoin the S.A.A. Section.
   No lorries are available.

7. 44th. Field Ambulance will arrange to collect Sick from units present location one hour after departure.

8. O/C Companies (including Bn. H.Q.) will detail a rear party of 1 N.C.O. and 6 men to clean up billets, latrines etc. These parties will be collected and marched to destination by an Officer to be detailed by O/C B. Coy.

9. Parade. Parade will be as follows:—
   A. Coy. On road outside billets 7 a.m.
   B. Coy. at 2 cross roads 100 yds. below Bn. Orderly Room 7 a.m.
   H.Qrs. do do do
   C & D Coys. on Road outside Billets 7.30 a.m.
   Transport on road adjoining Transport Lines 7.30 a.m.

   Transport and Companies will be ready to march off at the above times.

   Dress - Full Marching Order. Order of march D - C - A - B - H.Q. Transport.

   Cookers will accompany Companies.

'Continued overleaf.'

10. Officers' Valises. Officers' Valises will be ready punctually at the following times :-
    A. Coy. Outside Officers' Mess. 6 a.m.
    B. " do do
    C. & D. Coys. at Q.M.Stores 5.45 a.m.
    H.Q. 6 a.m. outside Headquarters Mess.

11. Route. Starting Point - Road Junction 400 yds. S. of C. in LE CLAYE at 8 a.m. - X roads ½ mile S. of Q. in QUINGOIE- AUDREHEM - BONNIQUES - TOURNEHEM (destination).

12. Tents. Tents will be stacked as follows :-
    A & B. Coys. 5.30 a.m. outside Battn. Orderly Room.
    C. & D. Coys. at Quartermaster's Stores 5.30 a.m.

13. REVEILLE   5 a.m.
    BREAKFAST.   5.30 a.m.

14. ACKNOWLEDGE.

[signature]
Capt. & Adjutant
18th. York & Lancs. Regiment.

Issued to all recipients of Operation Order No. 3.

SECRET. OPERATION ORDER No. 3/2 Copy No. ....
BY LIEUT. COLONEL L.R.JONES M.C. COMMANDING
13th. YORK & LANCS. REGIMENT.   Appendix 5

Ref. Map - HAZEBROUCK.   11.7.18.

1. In continuation of Battalion Order No. 3/1, the Battalion will continue to march to LES MARNIERES to-morrow, 12.7.18.

2. The instructions contained in para 4 of O.O. No. 3 will be complied with. O/C D. Coy. will detail a party of 1 Officer and 10 Other Ranks to march in rear of the Battalion to collect stragglers.
   (a) All Transport personnel will wear full marching order (drivers will not wear packs).
   (b) One Cook will march behind each cooker. The remaining personnel attached to the Transport will march as a formed party in rear of the Transport.

3. O/C Companies will render a Falling Out State as soon as possible after arrival in Billets.

4. The 5 G.S.Wagons from S.A.A. Section, D.A.C. will report to H.Q. D.A.C. after the Battalion arrives in new billets to-morrow.

5. O/C Companies (including Bn. H.Q) will detail a rear party of 1 N.C.O. and 6 men to clean up billets, latrines etc. These parties will be collected and marched to destination by an officer to be detailed by O/C D. Coy.
   These parties will report to the officer i/c rear party at Battn. H.Q. 9.30 a.m. 12.7.1918. The O/i/c Party will obtain a certificate before leaving from the Area Commandant to the effect that all billets etc. were left in a clean and sanitary condition.

6. PARADE.
   Parades will be as follows:-
   All Companies and Transport will parade on road outside their respective billets ready to march off by 8.30 a.m. 12.7.1918.
      Order of march - B,A,C,D, H/Q, Transport.
      Dress - Full Marching Order.
      Cookers will accompany Transport.

7. ROUTE.
   Starting point - Road junction ¼ mile N. of R. in TOURNEHEM at 9 a.m. - NORDAUSQUES - LES MARNIERES (destination).

8. MARCH DISCIPLINE.
   O/C Companies will ensure that files are changed after every halt.

9. OFFICERS' VALISES.
   Officers Valises will be stacked outside their Company H.Q. by 7 a.m. 12.7.18.

10.   REVEILLE.   6.0 a.m.
      BREAKFAST.   6.30 a.m.

11.   ACKNOWLEDGE.

                                        Capt. & Adjt.

Issued at 4.30 p.m. 11.7.1918 to all recipients of O.O. Nos. 3 and 3/1.

18th. YORK & LANCS. REGT.
RELIEF ORDER NO. X
BY LIEUT.COLONEL L.R.JONES M.C. COMMANDING.

18.7.18

1. 18th YORK & LANCASTER REGT. will relieve the 13th 'Fusiliers' in the DIFQUES Sub-Section on the night 18/19th July 1918.

2. ORDER OF RELIEF.
   A. Coy.18th Y & L will relieve 'B' Coy.13th Fus. in Right Front Coy.
   B Coy   do   do   'D' do 13th " . in Left Front Coy.
   C do   do   do   'C' do 13th " . in Support
   D do   do   do   'A' do 13th " . in Reserve.

3. GUIDES.
   One guide per platoon will meet the Battalion at Road Junction Q.21.a.2.0

4. ROUTE & ORDER OF MARCH.
   HOUILLE-DIFQUES Road.
   Companies will march in Platoons at 100 yds. interval in the order A,C,B,D,H/Q. 1st Platoon of 'A' Coy. to pass road junction Q.16.b.7.1. at 10 pm.

5. LOCATIONS TABLE.
   Battalion Headquarters Q.26.b.7.7
   A. Coy, H.Q. (Y. & L).............Q.20.b.3.2.
   B   do   do Q.20.c.5.4
   C   do   do   ....Q.20.d.3.1.
   D   do   do Q.27.a.7.7

Issued at 2 p.m. 18.7.1918

                                    Capt. & Adjt.
                                18th Battn. York & Lancs. Regt.

Issued to all Recepients of Relief Order W. of 29.6.18.

BATTALION NIGHT MARCHING SCHEME.

NOTES.
1. Strict March Discipline will be maintained throughout.
2. OsC. Companies will arrange to take L.G.Limber with Coy. These will be able to proceed to Coy. H.Q. where teams will unload and carry forward.
3. When platoons are reported to be in position (i.e. for deployment to posts) two runners will report to Battn. Head- quarters and will receive orders for the return march. On receiving these, Os.C.Coys. will send his platoons back at at least 100 yds. interval.
4. While waiting for the above orders Platoon Commanders will take their Platoons in Visual Training.
5. Tea will be served on return to Billets.
6. Four guides per Company and one for Bn. H.Q. will report to 2/Lt Mundy at Battn. H.Q. at 7-30 pm. to act as Guides. (Scouts will be sent as far as possible).

NOTES (CONTD).

4. While waiting for the above orders platoon Commanders will take their platoons in Visual Training.
5. Tea will be served on return to Billets.
6. Four guides per Company and one for Bn H.Q. will report to 2/Lt. MUNDY at Battn. H.Q. at 7.30 p.m. to act as Guides. Scouts will be sent as far as possible.

SECRET.   18TH BATTN. YORK & LANCS. REGT.

ADDENDUM NO.2 TO BATTN. ORDER NO.1 DATED 27/6/18   COPY NO.

1. Ref. Para 5 Addendum No.1 to B.O. No.1 dated 27/6/18. Major J.Foulkes D.S.O. will be in command of train X713 and not Capt. C.H.M.Owen, M.C.

2. OFFICERS' EQUIPMENT.   (a) All Officers warned for Service overseas who have not drawn equipment, will draw same from Q.M.Stores before 10 am. to-morrow, 2nd July.
    (b) Officers who are not proceeding overseas, and who are in possession of equipment will return same to Q.M.Stores by 10 am. 2/7/18.
    (c) All Camp equipment drawn by Officers from Q.M. will be returned to Store by 10 am. 2/7/18.

3. Blankets. All blankets, rolled in bundles of 10, will be stacked outside Q.M.Stores by 9 am. to-morrow, 2nd July.

4. The following Officers will not proceed overseas with the Battalion:-

Capt. A.O.Kaye	Capt. A.S.Bell
do H.H.Drabble	Capt. C.W.S.Scott
2/Lt G.H.Boddington	2/Lt E.Bailey
do A.Broomfield	do E.Hardy
do J.Bennett.	do R.E.Macfadyen.

Upon the departure of the Battalion, these Officers will come under the orders of Major Hayward, Commandant, Stoney Castle Camp, pending further instructions.

Issued to all recipients of Addendum No.1 to Battn. Orders, No.1 dated 27/6/18.

(Sgd) Basil H.Pickering,
Capt. & Adjt.
18th Bn. York & Lancs. Regt.

Stoney Castle Camp,
1./7/18.

SECRET.   18th YORKS. & LANCS. REGIMENT.   Copy No. 17

311/14

ADDENDUM No. 1 to BATTN. ORDER No. 1 dated 27.6.1918.

The following paras. of Battalion Order No. 1 dated 27.6.18 are cancelled :-, 1, 2, 5, 8.

1. The Battalion will entrain in accordance with attached Time Table.

2. Companies will detail a loading party for Vehicles of all Units of the Brigade as follows :-

A. Coy.	1 Sgt.	12 Men.	
B. "	1 Cpl.	12 "	
C. "	1 Cpll	12 "	
D. "		11 "	Total 50 O.R.

Lt. SKIDMORE is detailed as Officer in charge of this party. The party will report to R.T.O. BROOKWOOD STATION at 3 a.m. 1st. July.   Parade 2 a.m. 1.7.18.   Dress - Clean Fatigue.

Capt. T.A.BULLOCK will be responsible for entraining all Units of the 41st. Inf. Bde, both on 1st. July and 2/3rd July in accordance with attached Train table.

3. Two motor lorries will report at Q.M.Stores at 3 am. 1/7/18 for the conveyance of Officers' valices & Stores to the station. R.S.M. will detail loading party of 1 N.C.O & 8 men to report at the Q.M.Stores, 3 am. Officers' valices will be stacked outside Q.M.Stores by 3-30 am. 1/7/18. Lorries will be loaded and ready to move off by 5-30am. They will be required to be at Brookwood Station at 6-30 am 1/7/18. It must be clearly understood that all baggage & stores ex--cept personal property which can be carried must proceed by these lorries as no other Transport will be provided after the departure of the first line Transport of the Battalion.

4. Capt, D. Donne M.C. is detailed to proceed with Transport via Southampton. 2/Lt C.Leader B.T.O will also proceed on 1st July via Southampton and willl be responsible for supervising the embarkation of all animals at Southampton.

5. Parades will be as follows:-

Train X 301. Transport Coy. 5-15am. 1/7/18
Officer I/c Train Capt P.Donne, M.C.

Train X713   A Coy.   9-30 p.m.   2/7/18
              B Coy   do   do
              ½ H.Q. Coy   do   do
Officer I/c Train, Capt. C.H.M.Owen, M.C.

Train X714   C Coy   10 p.m.   2/7/18
              D do   do   do
              ½ H.Q. Coy   do   do
Officer I/c Train, Lt. Col. L R.Jones, M.C.

(2).

Addendum No. 1 (contd)

6. **Instructions regarding Entrainment.**
Units will be drawn up (head of column) 50 yards from entrance to Station 2 hours before then train is due to start.
On arrival of the Companies the Officer Commanding Train will report to R.T.I. on platform.
When the unit is ordered to move on to the platform , the following procedure will be adopted:-

(1). Men and horses will be marched to the platform and be formed up facing the trucks. Entrainment will commence at once (after horses have been told off to trucks and entrained) simultaneously from each end of the train (an average of 8 horses to a truck, 8 men to a compartment)

(2). Vehicles will be drawn up as the R.T.O. directs. Teams will be unhooked and led off to entrain.

(3). The loading party will stand to the vehicles (5 men to each four-wheeled vehicle) ready to man-handle them on to the trucks

(4) Baggage and supplies will be loaded by the baggage fatigue into the trucks indicated by the R.T.O.

(5). All hay and straw must be removed from vehicles and placed in brake-van, unless completely covered by a sheet.

(6). Rifles must not be left on vehicles, but taken into the compartmens by their owners.

(7) The commanding officer will inform the R.T.O on his unit see below is *completely entrained*.

7. Animals on charge of Brigade H.Q. will be entrained with Battalions one horse proceeding with each unit, so arranged that the total number on each train can be divided into batches of 8.

(Sgd) Basil H. Pickering Capt & Adjt
18th Battn York & Lancs Regt.

Stoney Castle Camp,
June 30th 1918.

Distribution.
1. Commanding Officer.
2 O/C A. Coy.
3 O/C B. Coy
4 O/C C Coy.
5 O/C D Coy.
6 Quartermaster
7 Transport Officer.
8 Capt Bullock
9 Lieut Bailey
10 R.S.M.
11 H.Q. 41st Inf. Bde.
12 War Diary
13 do
14 File
15 File
16 M.O.

item 9 Horses and mules, with the exception of pack animals, will be entrained harnessed, unless otherwise ordered
The Officers l/c trains will make out warrants for the whole train load for which they are responsible at the R.T.O's Office where warrant forms will be supplied.

Train No.	Coy.	Officers.	O.R.	Transport.	Baggage & Stores.	From	To	Starting Day.	Train departs.	Head of Column to reach Station.
X.301 TRANSPORT.		Capt. DONNE 2/Lt. Leader. " Reiley.	50	Horses & Mules 55 4 whld. Vehicles. 14 2 whld. Vehicles. 4 Bicycles. 9	5 Tons.	BROOK-SOUTH- WOOD.	1.7.18	9.30 am	6.30 am
X.713.	A. Coy. B. " ½ H.Q. Coy.		458			BROOK- WOOD	FOLK- STONE.	5.7.18	12.45 am	10.45 pm 2.7.18
X.714	C. Coy. D. " ½ H.Q. Coy. Bn. H.Q.		458			do	do	do	1.15 am	11.15 pm 2.7.18

30.6.18.

18th Bn. N.N.D. LdKR.

AMENDED.   Copy No. ....

Amendment to Addendum No.1. to Battalion Order No.1. d/27-6-18.
~~~~~~

1. Para. 3. Parades, is cancelled and the following substituted.
   Train No.713   Parade 10.30 p.m.   3-7-1918.
   Train No.714. Parade 11   p.m.   3-7-1918.

2. Last Column of Time Table "Head of Column to reach Station" is amended as follows:-

   Train No.713 for 11.45 p.m. read 11.45 p.m. 3-7-1918.
   Train No.714 for 12.15 p.m. read 12.15 a.m. 3-7-1918.

                                                (Sgd) B.H. Pickering.
                                                       Capt. & Adjutant.
                                                18th Bn. York & Lancs. Regt.
Pinbright.
3-7-1918.

Issued to all recipients of Battalion Order No.1. d/23-6-1918.

APPENDIX I.

193/14

SECRET.

Copy No. 13.

BATTALION ORDER No. 1 BY
LIEUT. COLONEL L. R. JONES M.C. COMMANDING
18th. YORK & LANCS. REGT.

1. MOVE.
The Battalion will entrain for abroad on the 30 June/1st July 28th. June, 1918. The entraining station and time will be notified later.

2. ENTRAINING PARTIES.
(a). Major D.C. HAMILTON M.C., D.A.Q.M.G. will be responsible for the entrainment of the Division. T. A. BULLOCK
(b) A/Capt. A.S. BELL is detailed to assist Major HAMILTON to entrain all troops belonging to this Brigade. This officer will report to Major HAMILTON at the entraining station four hours before the first train conveying troops of this Brigade is due to depart.

3. TRANSPORT.
Two Lorries will be provided to convey stores and baggage to the station.

4. SUPPLIES.
Rations for consumption on the day after entrainment will be taken.

5. HARNESS & SADDLERY.
On arrival at the Station, Harness & Saddlery will be placed in Sacks and labelled in order that it can be quickly obtained at the detrainment station. The Transport Officer will be responsible that this order is properly carried out.

6. WATER CARTS & WATER BOTTLES.
Water Carts and Water Bottles will be filled before entrainment.

7. ENTRAINMENT STATES.
Entrainment States will be rendered by O/C Companies and Transport Officer to the Orderly Room two hours before the time the Battn. is ordered to march out.

8. TIME OF ARRIVAL AT ENTRAINING STATION.
Transport will arrive at the Entraining Station 3 hours and the troops one hour before the train in which they are to travel is due to depart.
In order to avoid congestion at the entraining station Troops and Transport will be kept clear of the Station Yard until orders have been obtained from Major HAMILTON to enter the Yard.

9. ~~LEAVE.~~
~~All ranks will be in camp by 12 midnight 27/28th. June.~~

10. DRAFTS & REINFORCEMENTS.
All drafts arriving subsequent to 12 midnight on 27th. inst. for 41st. Infantry Brigade and S.A.A. Section, or 12 midnight 28th. inst. for Divisional H.Q. and 42nd. Infantry Brigade will be temporarily attached to 43rd Brigade until arrival in France when they will be handed over to their respective Brigades.

11. TRAIN TRANSPORT.
The Train Transport of the Battalion will join on arrival overseas.

12. DETAILS.
Lieut. E. BAILEY is detailed to take charge of all men left behind. He will be in possession of a nominal roll of all men left in his charge and will be required to know where every man is i.e. In Hospital, Camp. etc.
As soon as the Battalion entrains the above officer will come under the orders of Major W.G. HAYWARD, Commandant, StoneyCastle.

Battn. Order No. 1 (Sheet 2).

13. PERSONAL BELONGINGS.
   All surplus personal belongings and Kit will be sent to the men's own homes by the men concerned before to-morrow night 28th. June, 1918. O/C Companies are responsible that this order is brought to the notice of every man in their Company.

   The maximum weight of officers valises for overseas will be 50 lbs. Surplus Private belongings must be sent home prior to night of 28th. inst.

14. ACKNOWLEDGE.

Basil H. Pickering
Captain & Adjutant.
18th. York & Lancs. Regiment.

Issued at __11 am__
~~28~~.6.1918.
27

DISTRIBUTION.
1. Commanding Officer.
2. O/C A. Coy.
3. O/C B. Coy.
4. O/C C. Coy.
5. O/C D Coy.
6. Quartermaster.
7. Transport Officer.
8. Capt. BELL.
9. Lieut. BAILEY.
10. R.S.M.
11. H.Q. 41st. Inf. Bde.
12. War Diary.
13. War Diary.
14. File.
15. File.
16. M.O.

ORIGINAL.

Army Form C. 2118.

WAR DIARY

~~INTELLIGENCE SUMMARY.~~

(Erase heading not required.)

Vol 3

Confidential

War Diary

of

18th Battn. York and Lancaster Regiment

From 1st August, 1918 to 31st August 1918

(Volume 3)

Instructions regarding War Diaries and Intelligence Summaries are contained in F. S. Regs., Part II. and the Staff Manual respectively. Title pages will be prepared in manuscript.

Place	Date	Hour	Summary of Events and Information	Remarks and references to Appendices

Army Form C. 2118.

WAR DIARY
or
INTELLIGENCE SUMMARY.
(Erase heading not required.)

Place	Date	Hour	Summary of Events and Information	Remarks and references to Appendices
Moulle	1/8/18	7-30 am to 3-30 pm	Battalion training. Companies in attack & outposts. Gas Drill P.T. & A.G. Arm Drill, and Specialist training	
do	2/8/18	10-12.30 noon 9-3 pm to 12-30 pm	Firing of Bad Shots on Rifle Range Co-ordination March and attack on a French System. Being aid laying out defences and obstacles practised	
do	3/8/18	10-12 noon 2-4 pm	Demonstration on 'A' Range. Test of Gas efficiency by Div. Gas Officer Section Specialist training	
do	4/8/18		Church Parades 2/Lt R.S. Pickett and 24 Other Ranks represented the Brigade at a Special Parade Service held at TERDEGHEM in commemoration of the 4th anniversary of the War. After the service the whole of the Troops present at the service marched past His Majesty the King	
do	5/8/18		Divisional Horse Show at EPERLECQUES. The Battalion won the Divisional Commander's prize for the total number of marks	

Army Form C. 2118.

WAR DIARY
or
INTELLIGENCE SUMMARY.
(Erase heading not required.)

Instructions regarding War Diaries and Intelligence Summaries are contained in F. S. Regs., Part II. and the Staff Manual respectively. Title pages will be prepared in manuscript.

Place	Date	Hour	Summary of Events and Information	Remarks and references to Appendices
Moulle	6/8/18	8-30 am to 12-20 pm	Battalion firing on Range - Company Rifle Shooting Competitions. Specialist Training	
do	7/8/18	9-10 10-11	Platoon Inspection. Arms Drill, Musketry Demonstration by Special Platoon on Guard Mounting and Lewis Gun Drill	
		9-30 am to 12-30 pm	Battalion Practise Trench Relief & Gas Drill. Company H.Q. and 2 Platoons of "B" Coy proceeded to Malhove and provided guards for the safeguarding of important communications against sabotage. Coy H.Q. Malhove.	
do	8/8/18	8-30 am to	Platoon Inspection. Skeleton Training. Musketry and Lewis Gun classes	
		12-30 pm	P.T and Bombing Instruction. Specialist Training	
do	9/8/18	8-30 am to 4 pm	Musketry - Bombing, Lewis Gun and Specialist tests. Battalion Field Practice Competition - Company in attack on "A" Range	

WAR DIARY
or
INTELLIGENCE SUMMARY.

Army Form C. 2118.

(Erase heading not required.)

Place	Date	Hour	Summary of Events and Information	Remarks and references to Appendices
Moulle	10/8/18	8:30 am to 11:30 pm	Platoon Demonstration Attack	
do	11/8/18		Church Parade and Inspection of Billets. Major J. S. Foulkes D.S.O. being posted to R.A.F., Reading is struck off strength	
do	12/8/18	8 am to 4 pm	Musketry on Quarry Range. Platoon Training. Major J. U. Gunn Grey 10th West Yorks Regt. reported to units for duty 11/8/18 in view of his taking over command 12/8/13 in view of patrolers S.S.P.	
do	13/8/18	9 am to 12:30 pm	Companies — Bathing. Platoon Training, Section Training and firing on Quarry Range	
do	14/8/18	8:30 am to 12:30 pm	Ceremonial Drill. Platoon & Specialist Training	
do	15/8/18	8:30 am to 11:30 pm	Aeroplanes firing on "D" Range	

WAR DIARY
or
INTELLIGENCE SUMMARY.
(Erase heading not required.)

Army Form C. 2118.

Place	Date	Hour	Summary of Events and Information	Remarks and references to Appendices
Moulle	16/8/18	10.00	Companies to be formed well. Companies carrying out Company Deployment Tactics.	
do	17/8/18	9.am to 12	Musketry and Lewis Gun Recruits Tests. Demonstration Platoon on Guard drill & Ceremonial Describe. H1 st Infantry Brigade Minor & Short Competition. No 6 Platoon represented the Battalion, took second place in the event. T/g. C.M. Reed on W.S 360 - Lce A Simmons 2/Lt J Fell passed there fit for duty	
do	18/8/18		Church Parades and Inspection of Billets.	
do	19/8/18		Battalion preparing for move to new area. Bombing Demonstration of practice with live grenades. Transport preceded by advance party to WORMHOUDT and billeted. Three night 9:20 p August.	O.O. N° 14 attached marked "Off".7

WAR DIARY
or
INTELLIGENCE SUMMARY.

Army Form C. 2118.

Place	Date	Hour	Summary of Events and Information	Remarks and references to Appendices
Moulle	20/8/18		Battalion moved to Brass Camp St JAN TER BIEZEN. Battalion marched to HATTEN Station 9 am and entrained for PROVEN and from there marched to ROAD-CAMP. Move complete 3.0 pm. Remainder of Transports entrained at ST. OMER and detrained at PROVEN. O.O. No. 41 attached and marked. Capt. Fairplant B.M. Pickering became attached to H.Q. 2nd Inf. Bde H.Q. and took over duties of 2/ Brigade Major temporarily.	App. 8
St Jan Ter Biezen	21/8/18	9 am to 12.30 pm	Commanding officer's inspection of companies. Platoon training. Lewis gun & rifle classes.	
		2 pm	Lecture to all Platoon Commanders and N.C.O.'s on "Training of Sections"	
do	22/8/18	8 am to 12 noon	Battalion Drill. Rapid Deployment of companies. Platoon & Section training. 2/Lt W.A. Owens joined the Battalion for duty	

Army Form C. 2118.

WAR DIARY
or
INTELLIGENCE SUMMARY.
(Erase heading not required.)

Instructions regarding War Diaries and Intelligence Summaries are contained in F. S. Regs., Part II. and the Staff Manual respectively. Title pages will be prepared in manuscript.

Place	Date	Hour	Summary of Events and Information	Remarks and references to Appendices
ST JAN TER BUEZEN	23/3/18	8 am to 12 noon	Platoon in Tivet Movement Exercises, Section Training in Lectures. Information from Prisoners. One Company on 30 yds Range	
do	24/3/18	8 am to 12 noon	Platoon Training, Arm Drill, Guard Duties, Rapid Aiming, Section Rapid Loading Competition. One Company on Range	
do	25/3/18		Church Parades and Inspection of Billets	
do	26/3/18	8 am to 12 noon 2pm to 4pm	Platoon & Section Training. P.T & B.F. Night Operations, Section Patrolling under Platoon arrangements	

Army Form C. 2118.

WAR DIARY
or
INTELLIGENCE SUMMARY.
(Erase heading not required.)

Place	Date	Hour	Summary of Events and Information	Remarks and references to Appendices
ST. JAN-TER BIEZEN	27/8/15	9am	Battalion proceeded to Forward Area by Light Railway from Lancaster Camp J 19 a (28 N.W.4) detraining at KEMMELBEEK (28 N.W.7) and marched to SIEGE CAMP (B 26 F.1.9) Movement complete 5pm. O.O. No 5 attacked marked.	cbs 9
do	29/8/15		Battalion Resting. Battalion proceeded to the Trenches and relieved No 8 B Scottish Rifles in the Left Sub-Section of the Brigade Front from to Relief complete. Companies disposed as under:- A Coy in Reserve B do Left Front Coy C do Late do D do Right do O.O. No 5/1 attached + marked	app. 10

Army Form C. 2118.

WAR DIARY
or
INTELLIGENCE SUMMARY.
(Erase heading not required.)

Instructions regarding War Diaries and Intelligence Summaries are contained in F. S. Regs., Part II. and the Staff Manual respectively. Title pages will be prepared in manuscript.

Place	Date	Hour	Summary of Events and Information	Remarks and references to Appendices
L/b S.S. Sects. 29 8.19			The Battalion holding the line. Working parties were found by A Coy improving trenches. Front quiet. Hostile Artillery normal.	
do	30.8.18		Continued supplying Working Parties	
		10 PM	D Coy sent out a Patrol under 2/Lieut. WETHER who reconnoitred round WEST FARM, BOUNDARY FARM, and THATCHED BARN the base of enemy found.	
	30.8.18		Lt Col L R JONES M.C. C.O. proceeded on leave to UK. Major J McGAVIN-GREIG 2nd/L in command.	
do	31.8.18	1.30am	B Patrol. Left B Company lines under SNIDARE, and found the patrol, the right under 2/Lt HARBRON left C Company lines and	
		1.45pm	2/Lt Dunphy M Patrol under	
			proceeded to RAILWAY WOOD. There being found the patrol fired five rounds rapid on the enemy who fled. Patrol returned to about 6.30 am The Lieutenant sent a Brigade Commander sent the following compliments recognised upon his gallant work	

WAR DIARY
or
INTELLIGENCE SUMMARY

Army Form C. 2118.

Place	Date	Hour	Summary of Events and Information	Remarks and references to Appendices
Continued	31/8/18		"The B.G.C. congratulates 21st HUSSARS and the NCOs and men of his 'Patrol' on the efficient manner in which they carried out their duties on 31st August, 1918.	
			(Sd) Basil H. Rodney Capt. for G.S.O. Major 11 Infantry Brigade	
			The good work of the Division was acknowledged in a letter of congratulation from the Divisional Commander and the Brigade Commander as follows:-	

WAR DIARY
or
INTELLIGENCE SUMMARY.

(Erase heading not required.)

Army Form C. 2118.

Place	Date	Hour	Summary of Events and Information	Remarks and references to Appendices
Contained	31/8/18		"The G.O.C. desires to express his appreciation of the immense spirit shown by the Infantry of this newly raised Division during its first tour in the line" and "he wishes it to be explained to the troops that this Divisional spirit is" "having so the effect on the enemy, as expressed in prisoners with the ideas of our having further South. Even though it may not have been possible up to the present to register any very definite visible results." GSWAL RCC 2nd Bde "U Division"	May
			The B.G.C. who wishes to add his appreciation	Col. 6 Whickam Coyle? H. Du Boys H. Lefs. Bde

W.D.

APP. 7

SECRET.

COPY NO. 76

18th YORK & LANCASTER REGIMENT OPERATION ORDER NO. 4.

BY

Lieut. Col. L.R. JONES, M.C. Commanding. 18th August 1918.

Refce. Maps HAZEBROUCK 5A 1/100,000
27 - 1/40,000

1. The 14th Division (less Artillery) has been transferred from VII Corps to 11 Corps, and will move by Brigade Groups to the St. JEAN-TER-BIEZEN Area.
    On arrival in the New Area the 14th Division will be in 11 Corps Reserve.

2. The 41st Inf. Bde. Group will consist of the following Units:-

    41st Inf. Bde.
    15th L.N. Lancs Regt.
    89th Field Company R.E.
    44th Field Ambulance.
    No. 2 Coy. Div., Train.
    26th Mob. Vety. Section.

3. Personnel will move by train from WATTEN & St. OMER on 20th August, detraining at PROVEN for ROAD CAMP (27 F 25 d).

4. Transport will move by Road on 19th August in accordance with attached March Table "A".

5. The 26th Mob. Vety. Section will be attached to and will move under the Orders of No. 2 Coy. Div., Train from 19th August inclusive.

6. Marching Out State will be rendered by Transport Officer to Orderly Room by 8 p.m. to-night.

7. Transport Officer will render a Certificate to Orderly Room by 8 a.m. 19.8.18 that all Claims preferred against him by Owners of Billets have been settled.
    The Interpreter will obtain a "Certificate de bien vivre" from the owner of each Billet vacated.

8. Further Orders follow.

9. ACKNOWLEDGE.

Capt. & Adjt.
18th York & Lancaster Regiment.

Issued at.. 5.45 P.M.

DISTRIBUTION.

1. C.O.	12. R.S.M.
2. 2nd I/Command.	13. Area Commandant, MOULLE.
3. Adjt.	14. M.O.
4. O.C. "A" Coy.	15. Interpreter.
5. O.C. "B" Coy.	16. War Diary.
6. O.C. "C" Coy.	17. War Diary.
7. O.C. "D" Coy.	18. File.
8. 41st Inf. Bde.	19.
9. O.C. Signals	20.
10. Q.M.	21.
11. T.O.	22.

S E C R E T. TABLE "A" to accompany 18th YORK & LANCASTER OPERATION ORDER No. 4.

Date.	Unit.	From	To	Route.	Time of Starting.	Remarks.
August 19th.	18th Y.& L (Transport)	MOULLE	WORMHOUDT "B" Area	WATTEN ERKELSBRUGGE	To be clear of MOULLE by 8.30 a.m.	Billets from Area Commandt. WORMHOUDT.

APP. 8

SECRET.   COPY NO. 17
                18th YORK & LANCASTER REGIMENT OPERATION ORDER NO. 4/2.
                                  BY.
                    Lieut. Col. L.R. JONES, M.C. Commanding. 19th August /18.
Refce. Maps. HAZEBROUCK. 5A1/1,00,000
             27 - 1/40,000

1.   In continuation of Battalion Operation Order No. 4 the Battalion
     less Transport will entrain as under:-

Date.	Approx. Entraining strength.	Entrain at	Detrain at	Time train due to depart	Remarks.
20.8.18.	640	WATTEN	PROVEN.	9 a.m.	Probable duration of journey 3½ hours.

     On arrival in PROVEN the Battalion will proceed by Route March to
     ROAD CAMP 27/V.25.d.7.2.

2.   PARADES.
          The Battalion will parade in following order H.Q.Coy., "A","C","D"
     Coys, with head of column at junction DIFQUES-MOULLE & CALAIS Road.
     Dress:- Battle Order.

3.   LORRIES.
          2 Lorries are detailed for use of the Battalion, they will
     report at Q.M.Stores at 10 p.m. 19. 8. 18 and will do as many journeys
     as necessary.
          One Lorry for each Unit will meet trains on arrival at PROVEN
     and may be used to make as many journeys as necessary.

4.   OFFICERS VALISES. will be stacked outside Company H.Q. at 4 p.m.
     to-day 19.8.18 for collection by Transport. Mess Boxes will be
     delivered to Q.M.Stores by 9 p.m. 19. 8. 18.

5.   BLANKETS.
          Tightly rolled in bundles of 10 to be delivered to Q.M.Stores
     by 4 p.m. 19.8.18 An Officer will be responsible for the proper
     rolling of the blankets.

6.   SANDBAGS.
          Sandbags containing mens greatcoats and haversacks will be
     delivered to Q.M.Stores by 4 p.m. 19. 8. 18.

7.   COOKING UTENSILS.
          Except minimum required for Breakfast 20. 8. 18 will be delivered
     at Q.M.Stores by 6 p.m. 19. 8. 18.

8.   AREA STORES.
          Wash Bowls and Tents on charge of Companies will be handed to
     Q.M.Stores at 4 p.m. 19. 8. 18.

9.   RATIONS.
          Rations for the 20th August will be carried on the man.

10. WATER BOTTLES.
          Water Bottles will be filled with Lime Juice or water as desired.

11. O.C.Companies will render a Certificate to Orderly Room by 9 p.m.
     to-night. 19. 8. 18 that all claims preferred against them by Owners of
     Billets have been settled.
          The Interpreter will obtain a "Certificate de bien vivre" from
     the owner of each Billet vacated.

12. ACKNOWLEDGE.
                                            Capt. & Adjt.
                                            18th York & Lancaster Regt.
                                                P.T.O.

Issued. At........

Distribution.
```
 1. C.O.                12. R.S.M.
 2. 2nd I/Command.      13. Area Commandant, MOULLE.
 3. Adjt.               14. M.O.
 4. O.C. "A" Coy.       15. Interpreter.
 5. O.C. "C" Coy.       16. War Diary
 6. O.C. "B" Coy.       17. War Diary
 7. O.C.H.Q.Coy.        18. 2/Lieut. Letcher
 8. 41st Inf. Bde.      19. 2/Lieut. Kay
 9. O.C.Signals         20. Asst. Adjt.
10. Q.M.                21. File.
11. T.O.                22.
```

SECRET.
APPENDIX "A" TO OPERATION ORDER NO. 4/2.
18th YORK & LANCASTER REGIMENT%   19. 8. 18.

TRANSPORT.
In continuation of Battalion Operation Order No. 4/1 the remainder of the Transport will move on the 20th August 1918 as under:-

Vehicles.	Horses.	Personnel.
3 Lewis Gun Limbers	6.	3 Drivers.
2 Cookers (A & C Coys)	4	2 Drivers & 2 Cooks
2 Water Carts	4.	2 Drivers & 2 Water Duty men
1 Mess cart	1	1 Driver.
	11 Riding	11 Grooms
	6 Pack	6 Personnel.
		1 Transport Sergt.
		1 Transport Corporal
8	32	31

2/Lieut. E.S.LETCHER is detailed as Officer in charge of above.

The above will entrain at St.OMER at 8 a.m. 20.8.18 and will detrain PROVEN same day; probable duration of journey 3½ hours.

Parade ready to march off in Transport Lines 3 a.m. 20. 8. 18, report to R.T.O. St.OMER 5 a.m. 20. 8.18.

Transport Personnel will be responsible for the cleanliness of their own lines.

Water Carts and Water bottles will be filled before entrainment.

2/Lieut. M.R.KAY is detailed to assist the Staff Captain in entrainment at St.OMER and detrainment at PROVEN on 20th instant.

This Officer will report to Staff Captain at St. OMER STATION 4.30 a.m. 20th instant.

[signature]
Capt. & Adjt.
18th York & Lancaster Regt.

APP 9

SECRET.   13th. YORK & LANCASTER REGIMENT.   Copy No.
                    OPERATION ORDER No. 5.
                            by
            LIEUT.COLONEL L. RODWELL JONES M.C. COMMANDING.

Ref. Map. YPRES 1/10000 28 N.W.4.   26.8.1918.

1. PARADES.
        Reveille 5.30 a.m.
        Breakfast 6.15 a.m.

    The Battalion will parade at 9.0 a.m. on Battalion Parade Ground and will move off at 9.15 a.m. proceeding in the following order :-
Headqrs, A, B, C, D.
    Personnel will move by train from Lancaster Camp F.19.a, 11.0 a 27th. August, 1918, detraining at KEEM ELBEEK B.26.b.1.9.

2. DRESS.
    Battle Order, Water bottles filled (caps in sandbags).

3. BLANKETS.
    These will be carried on the man.

4. SANDBAGS.
    Sandbags containing men's Greatcoats, Haversacks and Soft Caps to be delivered at Q.M.Stores 8.0 a.m.

5. OFFICERS' VALISES.
    Officers' Valises will be stacked outside Q.M.Stores 7.30 a.m, also Mess Boxes for collection.

6. FIELD KITCHENS.
    Field Kitchens will be ready to move off at 7.30 a.m. with Boilers filled.

7. RATIONS.
    Haversack rations will be carried on the men.
    Tea Meal will be eaten at mid-day, dinners served on arrival at destination.

8. AREA STORES.
    Wash Bowls and Tents will be handed in to Q.M.Stores by 7.30 a.m.

9. O/C A,B,C,D, H/Q. Coys. and Transport Officer will render certificates to Battalion Orderly Room by 8.45 a.m. that Huts and Lines occupied by them have been left scrupulously clean.

10. ADVANCE PARTY.
    Lt. VINER and 1 N.C.O. from A, B, C, D, H/Q Coys. and Transport will report with Bicycles 8.0 a.m. at Brigade Headquarters St. JAN TER BIEZEN.

11. LEWIS GUNS.
    Lewis Guns and 20 Magazines per gun will be taken on trains and carried by men to destination. All surplus Lewis Gun Equipment other than these will be loaded on Company Lewis Gun Limbers by 7.30 a.m.

12. GUIDES.
    1/1st. HEREFORDS will arrange for Guides,- 2 per Coy. and 1 for Bn. H.Q. to be at KEMMELBEEK Station at 1 p.m. August 27th.

13. PLATOON DISTANCES.
    On Detraining a distance of 60 yards will be maintained between Platoons.

14. TRANSPORT.
    (1) Will move by road under Brigade Transport Officer to C.S.a.5.0.

O.O. No. 5 (SHEET 2);

14. TRANSPORT (CONTD).
(2). A Guide will meet them at A.23.a.4.0. at a time to be notified later.
Distance – 50 yds. will be maintained between each six vehicles.

15. FIELD KITCHENS & WATER CARTS.
These will proceed to SIEGE CAMP B.26.b.1.9. Horses will return to Transport Lines.

16. REAR PARTY.
Two men per Company and Headquarters will remain behind to clean up camp, and will form Loading Party for Motor Lorries.
2/Lt. B.A.CLARKE will be in charge of this Party.

17. MOTOR LORRIES.
Motor Lorries will report to Q.M.Stores for removing surplus stores 7.0 P.M, and proceed direct to SIEGE CAMP.

18. MARCHING OUT STATE.
Marching Out States will be rendered to Battalion Orderly Room by 9.0 a.m.

Chapman
2/Lieut. & Actg. Adjt.
13th York & Lancaster Regiment.

Issued at 11.50 P.m.
26.8.1918.

Distribution.
1. C.O.
2. Second in Command.
3. Adjutant.
4. O/C A.Coy.
5. O/C B.Coy.
6. O/C C.Coy.
7. O/C D.Coy.
8. O/C H.Q.
9. 41st. Inf. Bde.
10. O/C Signals.
11. Q.M;
12. T.O.
13. R.S.M.
14. M.O.
15. Lt. VINER.
16. 2/Lt. CLARKE.
17. War Diary.
18. War Diary.
19 & 20 Flis.

APP 10
File 114

S E C R E T.   18th YORK & LANCASTER ORDER NO. 5/1.   28th August 1918.
----

1. MOVE.
   The Battalion will relieve the 8th SCOTTISH RIFLES in the left sub-sector of the Brigade Section on night August 28/29.
   Companies of the 18th York & Lancs. will relieve corresponding Companies of the 8th Scottish Rifles as follows:-
   A. Coy. in Reserve.
   B. Coy. Left front Coy.
   C. Coy. Centre Front Coy.
   D. Coy. Right front Coy.

2. PARADES.
   Time of Parade 7.30 p.m. on the ELVERDINGHE-VLAMERSTINGE Road facing North.

3. ORDER OF MARCH.
   A.C.D.B. H.Qrs. Head of the column at SIEGE JUNCTION B.20.d.5.7 Platoons at 50 yards interval.
   Battalion will entrain at KEMMELBEEK SPUR 8.30 p.m. and Detrain at GOODRICH Station I.1.c.2.8. 9.15 p.m.
   On detraining Companies will proceed by ½ platoons, care being taken to keep connection.

4. GUIDES.
   One per Platoon and Coy. Headquarters, and two for Bn. Headquarters will be at GOODRICH Station 9.p.m.

5. DRESS.   Battle Order. Water bottles filled.

6. LEWIS GUNS. and 20 loaded magazines per gun will be man-handled.

7. REVOLVER AMMUNITION.
   All officers will be in possession of 24 rounds before leaving Indents to reach this Office by 5 p.m.

8. RATIONS. for August 29th will be carried on the man except tea, sugar and milk which will be taken up in sandbags.

9. WATER.
   Companies will take over 30 Petrol Tins (full) from Companies they are relieving.

10. COOKS.
    One Cook per Company. and Headquarters will be taken into the line.

11. BLANKETS.
    These will be rolled in bundles of 10 and dumped at Quarter Masters Stores by 5 p.m. to-night. An officer will supervise the rolling of blankets.

12. OFFICERS VALISES, MESS BOXES etc.
    To be in Quarter Masters Stores by 7.30 p.m. to-night.

13. SANDBAGS. (containing greatcoats and haversacks) will be dumped with Blankets at 5 p.m.

14. DETAILS.
    Battn. H.Qrs Administrative Portion and surplus Personnel will be in charge of 2/Lieut. NASON who will notify Companies as to edisposal of surplus Personnel to-night.

15. MARCHING-OUT STATE. will be rendered by 5 p.m.

Operation Order No. 5/1 Continued No. 2.

16. TRENCH STORES, etc.
Trench Stores, Defence Schems, Maps etc. will be taken over and receipts given. A list of Trench Stores taken over will be rendered to Battn. H.Qrs by 8 a.m. August 29th. Pro-formas attached.

17. COMPLETION OF RELIEF.
Will be notified to Battn. H.Qrs by the words
"GOODS RECEIVED".

18. ACKNOWLEDGE.

C. Robinson

2/Lieut. A/Adjt.
12th York & Lancaster Regiment.

Issued at. 4.45

Distribution.
1. C.O.
2. 2nd I/Command.
3. Adjt.
4. O.C.A.Coy.
5. O.C.B.Coy.
6. O.C.C.Coy.
7. O.C.D.Coy.
8. 41st Inf. Bde.
9. Signals.
10 O.C.H.Q.Coy.
11 Q.M.
12. T.O.
13. R.S.M.
14. M.O.
15. 2/Lieut. NASON
16. War Diary
17. War Diary
18 & 19 File.

ORIGINAL 31

Army Form C. 2118.

WAR DIARY
or
INTELLIGENCE SUMMARY.
(Erase heading not required.)

CONFIDENTIAL

WAR DIARY

OF

18TH YORK AND LANCASTER REGIMENT

VOLUME 4.

FROM 1ST SEPT 1918
TO 30TH SEPT 1918

WAR DIARY
or
INTELLIGENCE SUMMARY.
(Erase heading not required.)

Army Form C. 2118.

Place	Date	Hour	Summary of Events and Information	Remarks and references to Appendices
Ypres	1st.9.18	—	The Battalion on the line. Situation normal. Lt. Col. Forno L.P. M.C. left Batt: to take up duties as educational officer at G.H.Q. Major G. McEwen being left in temporary command of Batt:	M
Ypres	2nd.9.18	—	Battalion on the line. A daylight patrol of 1 officer and a platoon went out to Inasas in front of West Farm, they had established if Railway Wood, Horsejaw, and No man's land. Seeing no enemy were observed until 14.00 where the enemy were observed on the Cambridge Road. The patrol pushed forward until they were fired upon from Moatpost, they then returned. Two scouts pushed forward to Dilly Farm at 15.00 and discovered shell hole post 15.C.30.05 occupied by enemy at night, they were fired on and returned. Two patrols left our lines one for Dilly Farm 15.C.30.05 and the other went to Boundary Farm T.10.B.95.05: no trace of enemy were seen by either patrol.	M
Ypres	3rd.9.18	—	Two patrols went out. One to Hay Farm and Market Farm I.4.d. and one to Leo. Farm T.10.6. no trace of enemy were seen by either patrol.	M
Ypres	4th.9.18	—		
Ypres	5.9.18	—	Two patrols left our lines one to Market Farm I.4.d. no trace of enemy went seen by the other patrol visited Dilly Farm 15.C.20.05. a large party of the enemy were met but no encounter took place. A patrol of our officer and other ranks, guides proceeded by day to beyond West Farm and proceeded to Cambridge Road I.N.a.3.3. and were fired on the enemy m.g. from Moatpost. The patrol returned to Batt: at 12.00h. On the night of 5/6th Sept 1918 the Battalion were relieved by the 114th C.I.+ S.H. Regt.	M
Siege Camp	6.9.18	—	The Battalion entrained at Borovish Junction at 12.30 and detrained at Emmerasels Siege. for Siege Camp.	Ap?

Army Form C. 2118.

WAR DIARY
or
INTELLIGENCE SUMMARY.
(Erase heading not required.)

Instructions regarding War Diaries and Intelligence Summaries are contained in F.S. Regs., Part II. and the Staff Manual respectively. Title pages will be prepared in manuscript.

Place	Date	Hour	Summary of Events and Information	Remarks and references to Appendices
SIEGE CAMP	7.9.18	—	Battalion Training. Large working parties were formed for the R.E. Cleaning up.	
SIEGE CAMP	8.9.18	—	Platoon Training. Close order drill, Musketry, Physical Training, Bayonet Training, Rapid Loading, Owning Specialist Training. Large working parties were found for R.E.	
SIEGE CAMP	9.9.18	—	Platoon Training, Close Order Drill, Musketry, Fire Orders, Discipline, Rapid Loading and aiming, Physical + Bayonet training, Specialist Training. Large Working Parties were found for R.E.	
SIEGE CAMP	10.9.18	—	Platoon Training, Musketry, Specialist Training. Large Working Parties found for R.E.	
SIEGE CAMP	11.9.18	—	Platoon + Section Training, Musketry + Specialist Training. Working Parties found for Royal Engineers.	
SIEGE CAMP	12.9.18	—	Platoon and Section Training, Musketry + Specialist Training. Large working Parties found for R.E.	
SIEGE CAMP	13.9.18	—	Platoon + Section Training, Musketry + Specialist Training. The Battalion relieved the 14th Argyll + Sutherland Highlanders in the left section of the Bayenc Sub-Sector on the night of the 13th/14th Sept 1918. (Order no.) attached + marked — App. II	
YPRES SECTOR	14.9.18	—	Battalion in the line.	

Army Form C. 2118.

WAR DIARY
or
INTELLIGENCE SUMMARY.
(Erase heading not required.)

Instructions regarding War Diaries and Intelligence Summaries are contained in F.S. Regs. Part II. and the Staff Manual respectively. Title pages will be prepared in manuscript.

Place	Date	Hour	Summary of Events and Information	Remarks and references to Appendices
YPRES SECTOR	15.9.18	—	Battalion in the line. Situation quiet	
YPRES SECTOR	16.9.18	—	Battalion in the line. A.Coy pushed a post forward to Mill Hsse and remained there during the Batt" tour in the line. C.Coy pushed a post forward to James Farm and remained there until Batt" was relieved	
YPRES SECTOR	17.9.18	—	Battalion in the line. Situation quiet. One man wounded by explosive bullet. A patrol was sent out Lincoln James Farm to ascertain if the enemy had relieved, which was thought to be the case done so, but they were fired upon and retired.	
YPRES SECTOR	18.9.18	—	Battalion in the line. Situation normal.	
YPRES SECTOR	19.9.18	—	Battalion in the line. Battalion were relieved on the night of 19th-20th Sept by the 4th Seaforth Highlanders and proceeded to Billets at ST LAURENT (WINNEZEELE AREA) Order No 8 attached and marked.	App. III
ST LAURENT	20.9.18	—	Battalion Resting and Cleaning up Clothes, Equipment, Ammunition etc.	
ST LAURENT	21.9.18	—	Commanding Officers Inspection. Route March under Company arrangements.	
ST LAURENT	22.9.18	—	Church Parades. Batt" Bathing Parade at STEENVOORDE	
ST LAURENT	23.9.18	—	Batt" Training. Close Order Drill. Musketry. Physical & Bayonet Training. Major M.S Garvin Bray relinquished Support Command of Battalion on report of Lt Col Duncan M.C Returning duties of Commanding Officer.	

Army Form C. 2118.

WAR DIARY
or
INTELLIGENCE SUMMARY.
(Erase heading not required.)

Instructions regarding War Diaries and Intelligence Summaries are contained in F.S. Regs., Part II. and the Staff Manual respectively. Title pages will be prepared in manuscript.

Place	Date	Hour	Summary of Events and Information	Remarks and references to Appendices
ST LAURENT	24.9.18	—	Battalion Training. Close Order Drill, Musketry, Formation for Attack. Corps Commander visited Battalion during training.	
ST LAURENT	25.9.18	—	Battalion training. Close order drill, Formation for attack, Battalion Musketry.	
ST LAURENT	26.9.18	—	Battalion training. Close Order Drill. Gas training. Musketry. Formation for attack and Patrolling.	
ST LAURENT	27.9.18	—	The Battalion proceeded to found area at RENINGHELST the Brigade being in Divisional Reserve, for Operations. Parties were formed for duties in connection with Stragglers Posts, Escorts & Escorts for Prisoners.	
RENINGHELST	28.9.18	—	Battalion in Reserve for Operations which commenced on the 28th Sept. Parties formed as above.	
RENINGHELST	29.9.18	—	As for 28th Sept. Large quantities of Salvage were collected in the Area occupied by the Battalion.	
RENINGHELST	30.9.18	—	As for 28th and 29th Sept.	

Signature
LIEUT. COLONEL
COMMANDING 18th BN. YORK & LANCS REGT.

18 BN YORK & LANCS REGT. ORDER No 6

Sept 4th 1918

APP. I

Copy No:- 21

1 MOVE — The Battalion will be relieved by the 14th A & S H on the night of 5/6th Sept 1918.

    Entrain at <u>GOODRICH JUNCTION</u> at 12.30 am 6/9/18
    Detrain at <u>KEMMELBEEK SPUR</u> for SIEGE CAMP

    2/Lt J R Anderson will meet the trains conveying 14th A & S H at GOODRICH JUNCTION I/c 28 at 8.15 pm Sept 5th, and will be responsible for the entraining of Companies. He will report at the Batn Hd Qrs 7 pm 5/9/18 for instructions.

    Companies will proceed to entraining point immediately on relief.

    A distance of 50 yds will be maintained between half Platoons, care being taken to keep connection.

2 GUIDES — 2/Lt NASON will arrange for guides to be at detraining point to meet Companies.

    A B C D Coys will each detail 1 Guide per Coy HQ and 1 per platoon. OC HQ Coy will detail 2 Guides.

    The above will be at GOODRICH JUNCTION I/c 28 at 8 pm Sept 5th.

    They will report at Bn Hd Qrs 7 pm Sept 5th where Sgt Hutton will take charge of the party.

3 ADVANCE PARTY — 2/Lt FITTON B Coy and 1 NCO from A B C D & HQrs Coy will form an advance party to join 2/Lt NASON at SIEGE CAMP, to take over Camp and Shelters.

    They will report at Front Batt Ord Room at 12 NOON Sept 5th.

    2/Lt NASON will proceed from REAR HQrs with CQMS's from A B C D & HQrs Coys, and will be in Charge of Advance Party.

4 AREA STORES — All Area Stores at SIEGE CAMP will be taken over by 2/Lt NASON and receipts given.

P.T.O

CONTINUATION — ORDER No 6   4/9/18

5 TRENCH STORES — All permanent working parties, guards, AA posts, Defence Schemes, Aer photographs and Trench maps will be handed over on relief and receipts obtained from relieving unit.

Lists will be handed in to Batt Ord Room by 7pm 5/9/18

6 LIAISON POSTS — will be relieved by 7pm Sept 5th. Lt Yuner "B" Coy will be responsible for this relief

7 COMPLETION OF RELIEF — will be wired in BAB Code to this office

8 ACKNOWLEDGE

[signature]
Lt. Acting Adjutant
18 Bn York & Lancs Regt.

4/9/18

ISSUED AT

DISTRIBUTION —

1	C O
2	Adjt
3	A Coy
4	B
5	C
6	D
7	HQ
8	Signals
9	Bde
10	QM
11	TO
12	MO
13	2Lt Nason
14	2Lt Fitton
15	RSM
16	Sgt Dutton
17	14 A & S H
18	2d Belgian Gren
19 + 20	War Diary
20 + 21	File

SECRET. APP II

Copy No.

18th BATTN. YORK & LANCS. REGT. ORDER NO. 7

1. The Battalion will relieve the 14th A. & S. Highlanders in the left sub sector of the Brigade Section on the night, Sept. 13th/14th.
   Companies of the 18th York & Lancs Regt. will relieve the companies of the 14th A & S Highlanders as follows:-

A Coy.		Left front Coy.
B Coy.		In reserve.
C Coy.		Centre front Coy.
D Coy.		Right front Coy.

2. PARADES. Time of Parade 6-45 Pm. on the ELVERDINGE VLAMERSTINGE ROAD, facing North.

3. ORDER OF MARCH. A Coy., C, D, B and H.Q. Companies. Head of the column at SEIGE JUNC. B 20.d 5.7. Platoons at 50 yards interval. Battalion will entrain at KEMMELBEEK S-UR, B 20.b.1.7, 7-30 Pm. and detrain at GOODERICH, I 1 c 2 8 at about 8-15 Pm. On detraining Platoons will proceed by ½ Platoon, care being taken to keep connection.

4. GUIDES. One Per Platoon and Coy. H.Qrs and 2 Per Battalion H.Qrs will be at GOODERICH STATION at 8-15 Pm.

5. DRESS. Battle Order. Water bottles filled.

6. LEWIS GUNS. Lewis Guns and 20 loaded magazines Per gun will be man-handled. All surplus L.G. equipment will be dumped Battn. H.Qrs by Companies at 3 Pm.

7. REVOLVER AMMUNITION. All Officers will be in Possession of 24 rounds before leaving. Indents to reach this office by 3 Pm. to day.

8. RATIONS. Rations and water for Sept. 14th will be carried under Coy. arrangements.

9. COOKS. 2 cooks Per company and 1 cook, H.Qrs Coy. will be taken into the Line.

10. BLANKETS. These will be rolled in bundles of 10 and dumped at Battn. H.Qrs by 2-30 Pm. Sept. 13th. An Officer will supervise the rolling of blankets.

11. Officers' Valises and Mess boxes. To be at Battn. H.Qrs by 5 Pm. Sept. 13th

12. SANDBAGS. Sandbags (containing haversacks, caps & greatcoats) will be dumped with blankets at 2-30 Pm.

13. DETAILS. Battn. H.Qrs Administrative Portion and surplus Personnel will be in charge of 2/Lt Fitton, who will arrange for disposal of surplus Personnel. Details later.

14. MARCHING OUT STATE. Will be rendered to Battn. Orderly Room by 6 Pm. Sept. 13th.

15. LIAISON. O.C. A Coy. will arrange for 2 runners for duty with the Right front Company Belgian Battalion. The above will report at 42nd Inf. Brigade H.Qrs, H 5 b 2.4 at 10 am to day.

16. O.C. H.Qrs. Will arrange for 1 bugler to relieve 14th A & S Highlanders bugler at SALVATION CORNER I 1 d 0 8.

17. SIGNALLERS. Will Parade as ordered under R.S.M. 12-30 Pm. Sept. 13th.

18. REAR PARTY. 2/Lt Clarke will arrange to hand over Camp Stores & Defence Schemes &c, obtaining signature for same. He will hand over receipt to 2/Lt Fitton, O.C. Details.

18th Battn. York & Lancs. Regt. Order No. 7 (contd)

19. COURSES. All Officers, N.C.Os and men Proceeding on courses as detail-ed in Battn. Orders will not be taken up the Line.

20. TRENCH STORES. Trench Stores, Defence Schemes, Maps &c will be taken over and receipts given. A list of Trench stores taken over will be rendered to Battn. H.Qrs by 8 am. Sept. 14th. Pro formas attached.

21. COMPLETION OF RELIEF. Will be notified to Battn. H.Qrs by B.A.B. code

22. ACKNOWLEDGE.

C. Robinson

Sept. 13th 1918

2/Lt Acting Adjutant,
18th Battn. York & Lancs. Regt.

DISTRIBUTION.

1 C.O.
2 Adjutant.
3. O.C. A Coy.
4. O.C. B Coy.
5 O.C C Coy.
6 O.C D Coy.
7 O.C. H.Q Coy.
8 Brigade.
9 Signals
10 M.O.
11 Q.M.
12 T.O.
13 R.S.M.
14 Assistant Adjt.
15 2/Lt B.A.Clarke.
16X 14th A & S Highlanders.
17 Belgian Regt.
18 W.D.
19 W.D.
20 File
21 File.

SECRET   18th BATT. YORK AND LANCS REGT.   Order No:-8 Copy No:-

Reference Map Sheet 28.   Sept 19th 1918.

1. On night 19th/20th Sept 1918 the 41st Inf. Bde will be relieved in the YPRES Sector by the 26th Inf. Bde and the 87th Inf. Bde.

2. Companies and Batt. H.Q. will be relieved as follows:-
Right Front Coy 18th York and Lancs. by 7th Seaforth Hds 26th Bde.
Centre, Left Front, Support Coy, and Batt. H.Q. 18th York & Lancs by 8th Black Watch 26th Infantry Brigade.

3. The relief will be completed by 3 a.m. 20th inst.

4. Guides from 18th York and Lancs. as under will report at Batt HQ. at 5 P.m. today.
    1 Per Coy. Headquarters.
    1 Per Platoon.
    2 Per Batt. Headquarters.

X. 2/Lt Nason is detailed in charge of these guides and will report at time and Place as above.

5. All Permanent Working Parties, Guards, A.A. Posts, Defence Schemes, Air Photos, Trench Maps and Stores including PETROL TINS, will be handed over and receipts forwarded to Brigade Headquarters. Maps on the establishment of units will not be handed over.

6. Liaison duties and Posts will be relieved by the incoming Battalions.

7. S.O.S. Bugle Posts will be relieved by the incoming Battalions.

8. On relief the Battalion will proceed to the WINNIZEELE Area by Light Railway and will entrain as follows:-
11-30 P.m. Sept 19th at GOODFICH 28/I 1.c.1.8. detrain at MAURENT 27/K 19 a.8.5.
The Assistant Adjutant will supervise entrainment

9. The Battalion will be located in the New Area as follows:-
27/K 14.c.0.9.(Billets taken over from 14th A & S Hdrs)

10. Completion of relief will be wired in B.A.B. Code.

11. Acknowledge.

                                      Capt. & Adjt.
                                      18th Batt. York and Lancaster Regt.

ISSued at:-
   DISTRIBTION.
   1. C.O.   10. M.O.
   2. Adjt.   11. 2/Lt. W. P. Nason.
   3. "A" Coy.   12. R.S.M.
   4. "B" Coy.   13. 7th Seaforth Hdrs.
   5. "C" Coy.   14th 8th Black Watch.
   6. "D" Coy   15. Belgian Liaison Officer.
   7. H.Q.Coy.   16. War Diary
   8. Signals.   17. File
   9. Brigade.

Army Form C. 2118.

WAR DIARY
or
INTELLIGENCE SUMMARY.

(Erase heading not required.)

Instructions regarding War Diaries and Intelligence Summaries are contained in F. S. Regs., Part II. and the Staff Manual respectively. Title pages will be prepared in manuscript.

Place	Date	Hour	Summary of Events and Information	Remarks and references to Appendices

CONFIDENTIAL

WAR DIARY
of
1/4th Year and Lancaster Regiment

From 1st October, 1918   To 31st October 1918

Lawrence 5

WAR DIARY
INTELLIGENCE SUMMARY

(Erase heading not required.)

Army Form C. 2118.

Instructions regarding War Diaries and Intelligence Summaries are contained in F.S. Regs., Part II. and the Staff Manual respectively. Title pages will be prepared in manuscript.

Place	Date	Hour	Summary of Events and Information	Remarks and references to Appendices
OUDERDOM	1 Dec		Battalion moved from Ouderdom to Messines Ridge in support. No casualties on march.	
MESSINES	2 Dec		Battalion in support at Messines.	
"	3 Dec		No.	
"	4 Dec		1 OR wounded.	
"			Bani & Coy went up to an engineers fatigue + 3 OR's in support.	
"	5 Dec		Battalion relieved 19th & 1st Batn East. on Messines Front 3 Coys in front line R & B Coys, 1 in support. All movement from R.R. Riccard (1) all movement by night.	
"			D Coy returned to billet about 4.30am. R & B. took over M.R. 12 & market sector. A Coy D Coy were in reserve at R. Riccard. 1 OR wounded.	
MESSINES	6 Dec		Fairly quiet and normal on the front held by the Batn v.g. Patrols out nightly. No movement on the enemy's front. 2 OR wounded.	
"	7 Dec		Coy relieved C Coy in support in the M.R. v.g. No J O in reserve. Nothing front, 3 OR wounded.	

WAR DIARY
or
INTELLIGENCE SUMMARY.
(Erase heading not required.)

Army Form C. 2118.

Instructions regarding War Diaries and Intelligence Summaries are contained in F. S. Regs. Part II. and the Staff Manual respectively. Title pages will be prepared in manuscript.

Place	Date	Hour	Summary of Events and Information	Remarks and references to Appendices
COMINES	9th Oct		Patrols sent out to secure information of enemy which had were manoeuvring.	
do	10th		8 Coy brought forward fresh ammunition & 3 Platoons of enemy's infantry.	
do	11th		C Coy sent out to do work of entry to 3rd Brigade.	
do	12th Oct		Battalion retired by 2nd & C Coy and moved to support at LINDHART FARM. 7.2.31. to 1032. C in No 14 platoon under command BPW JONES.	
do	13th Oct		Battalion employed as a support to the GARHWAL RIFLES & their response.	
do	14th Oct		AB S.BB retired from PKS and returned to former billets. Battalion went in support (reserve) & 2nd GREEN HOWARDS at R. Surveille.	
	15 Oct		Battalion moved to Roune. Arrived at 3.15 pm billet in HAVET. Remainder Billet in WILLEMIN.	

WAR DIARY
or
INTELLIGENCE SUMMARY

Army Form C. 2118.

Place	Date	Hour	Summary of Events and Information	Remarks and references to Appendices
MERVILLE	16.4.18		Battalion still holding the line in front of MERVILLE	
do	17th	7.0	do	
HAZEBROUCK & LA FACTORIE	18.4.18		The Battalion marched from MERVILLE area to HAZEBROUCK area — a long march via OUTTERSTEENE — FLETRE — METEREN — FLETRE — with very short rests. Route taken past LA MOTTE au BOIS — BORRE — ST SYLVESTRE CAPPEL — TERDEGHEM	
RENCH	19.4.18		The Battalion marched from HAZEBROUCK area to RENCH area via CASSEL. Route taken HAZEBROUCK — ST SYLVESTRE — BAVINCHOVE — NOORDPEENE — BOURBECQUE — BUYSCHEURE — RENCH	
RUMER	20.4.18		The Battalion marched from RENCH area to HERZEELE area via CAESTRE. Route taken was via RENCH — ST MARIE CAPPEL — BAVINCHOVE — LUDERNE — MOUSERON — LUDERNE — BUYSCHEURE — MERCKEGHEM — BOLLEZEELE — HERZEELE ...	

WAR DIARY
or
INTELLIGENCE SUMMARY

Army Form C. 2118.

Place	Date	Hour	Summary of Events and Information	Remarks and references to Appendices
Bramshott	21st Oct		Cleaning up equipment, Clothes, Iron grease etc.	
do	22nd Oct		Company Training Two Orders Drill, Trotting PT.	
do	23rd Oct		Company Training One hour Drill, musketry PT, Lecture on Discipline, 3 hours Batallion at Training.	
do	24th W.S.		Company Training Two hours Drill, musketry Bayonet PT.	
do	25th Oct		Company Training Musketry PT, Bayonet on Rifle exercises warrant one hour Drill.	
do	26th Oct		Company Training Musketry PT, Lecture on Review of Troops. Company Drill, Musketry PT, Lecture from two Officers.	
do	27th Oct		Church Parade. Recreation and Training.	
do	28th Oct		Company Musketry PT, one hour Drill	
do	29th Oct		do	
do	30th Oct		do	
do	31st Oct		The Battalion hereleft into the Army ?? ?? ?? ?? ?? for the Front. ?? ?? With Britle Brand as Escort, ?? ?? ?? ?? ?? ??	

SECRET   21.

APP I

18th BATTALION YORK & LANCASTER REGIMENT   Copy No
ORDER No 10
by
Lieut Colonel C A DUNCAN Commanding

Sheet 28   1st Octr 1918

1. The Battalion will move into Forward Area this morning

2. **Route**
LA CLYTTE - KEMMEL - WYTSCHAETE

3. Time of Parade will be notified later

4. Companies will be prepared to move complete not later than 9 a.m. to-day

5. Trench Shelters and Officers kits will be sent to Battalion H.Q. by 7 a.m. this morning

6. O/C A Coy will detail a Loading Party of 1 N.C.O. and 10 men to report to Q.M. Stores at 6.45 a.m. rationed for to-day

7. **Advance Party**
Advance Party consisting of 2Lt A. Swift "A" Coy and 1 N.C.O. per Coy and Battn H.Q. will report at Battn H.Q. at 7 a.m.
Transport Officer will detail mounted Orderly to report as above to accompany party

8. Picks and shovels issued to the men will be dumped at Battn H.Q. by 7 a.m. this morning. Sandbags and Grenades will be carried on the man

Issued at 5.30 a.m. 1.10.18   (Signed) Basil H. Pickering
Issued to all recipients of Order No 9.   Capt & Adjt

SECRET   R   APP IV

            18th York & Lancaster Regt.
Ref. Sheet
Comines 1/40,000   Order No. 12

(1) The following alteration in the Inter-Battalion boundary of 41st Inf. Bde. Sector will be effected during the night 6/7 October 1918 and will then run from junction of WARNETON—COMINES railway with YPRES—COMINES canal in P36 c 45 90—P34 c 65 35, thence to River LYS at V4 b 10 00 (2) D Coy. will move from Support into the front line on the left of the Battalion Sector tonight. A Coy. will move into the accommodation evacuated by D Coy.
(3) From tonight Coy. frontages will be as follows:-

Right Front Coy. (C Coy) BAS-WARNETON crossroads V1c) b-c 1 inclusive to CEOGEE farm V1a 8 b 8 9 inclusive. Centre Front Coy. (B Coy) (inclusive) CEOGEE farm exclusive to pill boxes V3 b 20 55. Left front coy (D Coy) pill boxes V3 b 26 inclusive to left Battalion boundary V4 a 8 9 inclusive. Left front coy will establish the combined liason post with the 3rd Cdn. Regt at or about V4 a 8 9. O/C left front coy will notify Batt. H Q of exact location of this post when established.

(4) The above dispositions will be completed by 08 00 on the 7th inst.

(5) The 3 front line coys will forward sketched showing dispositions to Batt H Q by noon the 7th inst.

Acknowledge

6/10/18

Haul M. Lewis Capt & Adjt

S E C R E T   18th York & Lancs.   Order No 14.   APP 3

ref. map sheet 28 S.W.& S.E. 1/20,000

1. The 33rd London Regt will relieve the 18th Y & L Regt on the night 12/13th October 1918, in the Right subsector of the 41st Infantry Bde Sector. No movement will take place before 18.15.

2. RELIEF. Coys will be relieved as under:-
    A. Coy 33rd L.R.B. will relieve A. Coy 18th Y & L right front Coy.
    B. Coy   "   "   "   B. Coy   "   centre front Coy.
    C. Coy   "   "   "   C. Coy   " LEFT front Coy.
    D. Coy   "   "   "   D. Coy   "   Support Coy.

3. GUIDES. Companies will provide 5 guides to be at following Locations:-

        A Coy. ESPERANCE CART.   O 36 b 38   Time 1845.
        B Coy. CIRCLE FARM.   P 31 c 5 8   1845.
        D Coy. CIRCLE FARM.   P 31 a 58   1930.
        C Coy. VAUXHALL FARM.   P 32 b 55   1830.

5 Guides per Coy. found by the 33rd L.R.B. will be at PONT MAIRET P 31 b 45.

H.Qrs 18th Y & L will be located at GAPPARD FARM O35a.

4. LEWIS GUNS will be man-handled.
    Receipts will be obtained for ammunition etc. handed over.

5. Relief complete will be notified in BAB Code.

6. ACKNOWLEDGE.

                                          C Robinson Lt
                                               A/Adjt.

12/10/18.
1. C.O
2. 2nd i/c
3. Adjutant
4. A Coy.
5. B Coy.
6. C Coy.
7. D Coy.
8. H.Q. Coy.
9. Q.M.
10. R.S.M.
11. Welsh Fus.
12. D.C.I.
13. 33 Lon.
14. Sig. Off.
15. 41st Bde.
16. War Diary
17. File.

app 4

MAP SHEET
OBSE 1/20000

Staff Amendments
Orders No 18 Copy No

(1) MOVE
The Battalion will proceed by march route to RONCQ on today 19.10.8

(2) ROUTINE
Reveille 0530
Breakfast 0600
Parade 0715
Head of Column moves off 0750

(3) ROUTE Roads Junction Q32 a 33 – BOUSBECQUE – CUBA CROSS – (NGC34) RONCQ

(4) Parade The Battalion will parade outside Billets and will move off in the following order. II A HQ B C

Head of the Column will pass starting point (Roads June) Q32 a 33 at 0800

All movement will be by companies, at 200 yards ...... distance ...... will be maintained between vehicles. Halts will take place at 10 minutes past and 10 minutes to the clock hour.

(5) BILLETING PARTY
"C" Company will detail an officer to take charge of the billeting party of 1 NCO per Company and HQ and transport. To be detailed by Companies. The party will parade at Batt HQ at 0545 and report to A/Staff Captain at X8c 0560 at 0815

(6) RATIONS will be delivered to transport lines on completion of march. NO QM will detail a guide to be at Road Junction X8c 0560 at 1200 to meet the supply wagons.

OC A B C D Coy will make their own arrangements regarding their Company rations.
OC C Coy will also arrange to look for HQ during the march. Each man of HQ Coy will carry his own ??? rations.

continued overleaf

(7) TRANSPORT

No extra transport can be provided
First line transport will rejoin unit on completion
of march. The Billeting Officer and one N.C.O
from transport section will arrange necessary
accommodation.

Transport will move as follows:-
COMINES - WERNICQ SUD - BOUSBECQUE - CUBA CROSS
(NGC 34) RONCQ

Time to pass starting point X roads F28C9515
at 0900

Cookers + G.S. limbers will accompany the Battalion

(8) Instructions as to BILLETING in TOWNS

In Division SG Bring 18/10/18 as relating to
above are binding moved to all concerned

(9) 1 Runner from each company will report
location to Battalion H.Q. on completion
of move

(10) ACKNOWLEDGE

                                    Chotmorski
                                        L/t/y

ISSUED AT 0215 19/10/18

DISTRIBUTION
 1 C O
 2 OC A
 3 OC B
 4 OC C
 5 OC D
 6 I. O. Coy
 7 Transport Officer
 8 QM
 9 RSM   Chief Dermott
10 H. Rdc
11 W. Diary

SECRET.   18th YORK & LANCASTER REGIMENT.   Copy No......

ORDER NO. 20

Sheets 29 & 37   31.10.18

1. **MOVE.** The 18th York & Lancaster Regiment will relive 16th Manchester Regiment in the Right Battalion Front of the Right Brigade in the night of 31st October/1st November 1918. The relief to be complete by 00.01 1st November.

2. **GUIDES** Guides at the rate of 1 per Coy Headquarters, 1 per Platoons and 2 for Battalion Headquarters will be at 37/C.1.a.2.9 at 19.30

3. **RELIEF** Companies will relieve in the following order:-

    C Coy - Right Front Coy.
    D " - Left Front Coy.
    A " - Right Support.
    B " - Left Support. "

    Location of Batt. Headquarters is 29/U.26.c.9.7.

4. **TRENCH STORES.** All Defence Schemes, Aeroplane Photos, Maps, Trench Stores etc., will be taken over and receipts given. A list of Trench Stores etc. taken over will be forwarded to Battn. Headquarters by 09.00 on 1st November. A supply of forms for this purpose is issued herewith.

5. **DISPOSITION MAPS.** Companies will forward a map by 12.00 1st November showing their dispositions by posts.

6. **ORDERS TO O.C.T.M.B.SECTION.**
    These will be issued later.

7. **TRANSPORT LINES.**
    Transport Lines of the 16th Manchester Regt will be taken over. All Stores will be moved by Regimental Transport.

8. **COMPLETION OF RELIEF**
    Relief complete to be reported by B.A.B.Code.

9. **PARADES**
    The head of the Battalion will pass the Cross Roads in 37/A.10. c.8.7 at 16.00; 100 yards between Platoons in the following order: H.Qrs - D Coy - C Coy - B Coy - A Coy.
    Lewis Gun limbers will move with Companies.
    A halt for half hour will be made at the HERSEAUX aerodrome in 37/A.6.c. for tea.

10. **BILLETS**
    All billets will be left clean and tidy.

11. **ACKNOWLEDGE.**

Issued at 11.00
31.10.18

2/Lieut.
A/Adjutant.
18th York & Lancs Regt.

Copies to -
C.O.	H.Q.	R.S.M.
Adjt.	M.O.	Bde H.Q.
O.C. "A" Coy	Q.M.	War Diary
O.C. "B" "	T.O.	War Diary.
O.C. "C" "	Int.Offr.	File.
O.C. "D" "	O.C.T.M.B. Section.	File.

Original.

Army Form C. 2118.

WAR DIARY
or
INTELLIGENCE SUMMARY.
(Erase heading not required.)

Confidential
War Diary
of
18th York and Lancaster Regt.

From 1/11/1918.
To 30/11/1918.

Volume 6.

Army Form C. 2118.

WAR DIARY
or
INTELLIGENCE SUMMARY.
(Erase heading not required.)

Instructions regarding War Diaries and Intelligence Summaries are contained in F.S. Regs., Part II. and the Staff Manual respectively. Title pages will be prepared in manuscript.

Place	Date	Hour	Summary of Events and Information	Remarks and references to Appendices
ESPIERRES	1/11/18		Battalion on move on River ESCAULT in front to front ESPIERRES from HELCHIN 37/0.9.3.3 to 37/04.3.55. C & D in line at R/Front and Centre. B Coy - Left Left at Reserve. At 8.690 in Reserve. 2/LT J MUNDY took over in place of regiment and 2/LT A.F. GLADMAN to hospital.	[sig]
do	2/11/18		Battalion in line. Enemy artillery very active, many working enemy shells.	[sig]
do	3/11/18		Battalion in line. Enemy intermittent shells & machine gun fire on entrances of the batteries and the army shells + enemy.	[sig]
do	4/11/18		Battalion attacked at 5.40 a.m. Bank by taking ground to the line strongly KIR & 37/O M.36. from M98 (R.O.) Gorman left tunnel at 37/I Q & F & B enemy found camp and HELCHIN - REJET - AMOUGIES Road. R. BRAY who sent out to reserve and reform on entering attack at C.5.a. 20.05. Capt. GOODWIN RMRC, V.S.A Army Medical Mess came to Hospital at J.C. LOWDEN Rand look over RMRC, M.O. LT-COL. G.A. DUNCAN M.O. came over to Hospital. CAPT G.W. JEFFERSON took command of Battalion	[sig]

WAR DIARY

INTELLIGENCE SUMMARY

Army Form C. 2118.

Place	Date	Hour	Summary of Events and Information	Remarks and references to Appendices
ESPIERRES	8/11/18		37/C.16.a.70.55. Battalion in line. H.Q. & 2 platoons of "D" Coy at WATTRELOS 12th Suffolks on the right. 43rd Brigade relieved us with 15th R.W.F. at WATTRELOS in 37A.u. Party B also moved to be taken over. 2nd platoon of "A" Coy was moved and marched back. O.O. No 22 attached and marched O.O. No 23 attached	[signatures]
WATTRELOS	9/11/18		Battalion out of the line at disposal of Company commanders for purposes of training and re-equipping	JAL
do	10/11/18		Church Parade. C/E Events attended service from C of E at 9am. Service by Rev R.C. Rutherford (C.H.B Chaplain)	JAL
do	11/11/18	0900-1230	Ranks under Company arrangements. Formations of Arms &c. armistice of the enemy	JAL
	1430		Thanksgiving Service to celebrate the armistice of the enemy	JAL
do	12/11/18	0900-1230	Battalion Bathing &c. Parades under Company arrangements. Arms order and musketry. Stand to Rifle exercises. Specialists training under Specialist Instructors	JAL
	1400-1600		Supervised Games	

Lt. K. HARBROW took command of "E" Coy no from 11/11/18 vice 2/Lt. M.K.R.95

WAR DIARY
or
INTELLIGENCE SUMMARY.

Army Form C. 2118.

Place	Date	Hour	Summary of Events and Information	Remarks and references to Appendices
WATTRELOS	13/11/18		Battalion in reserve. G.O.C. Commander of B.D.G. reconnaissance for advance of Regiment northwards.	
	14/11/18		Battalion moves from WATTRELOS to BUNDUES via Nouveau through RUBAIX and NOUVAUX. O.O. 24 attached and marked route movements.	App II
BUNDUES	15/11/18	0900 1100 1400	Coy. Parade under Coy. Commanders. Ws. Inspection of Battalion Arms. M.C. its chars and ammunition of armoured cars movements.	
do	16/11/18	1000 1400	B.S. Co. Inspection of Battalion armoured Cars.	
do	17/11/18		Church Parade. B of O. Hon Capt. R.P.C.	
do	18/11/18	0900 1230 1400	Coys. at disposal of Coy Commanders. A.C. Inspector held by G. Coy. R.G.C class under R.S.L. Gajendrakumar.	
do	19/11/18	1030	G.O.C. Inspection of Brigade. Brigade Reviewed by General.	

Army Form C. 2118.

WAR DIARY
or
INTELLIGENCE SUMMARY.
(Erase heading not required.)

Instructions regarding War Diaries and Intelligence Summaries are contained in F. S. Regs., Part II. and the Staff Manual respectively. Title pages will be prepared in manuscript.

Place	Date	Hour	Summary of Events and Information	Remarks and references to Appendices
BONDUES	20/4/18	8.00	Classes under Rifle Bombers under by arrangement	
		9.00	Battalion engaged upon subject Demolition of Enemies	
		10.00	house to house.	
		11.00	Officer not engaged at its Coy Sgt Bombers officers super till 10.30 come in	
		1.00	the cook gallery.	
		1.30		
do	21/4/18	9.30	Coy at disposal of Coy Commander	
		10.00	Bombers Class.	
		11.00	Gallery including ? the Ranger's parades met with T.S.S. personnel gun 25 yds Bomb	
			Section.	
			To be C. below to the certain August. England C.O. Colonel	
do	22/4/18	9.00	Coy at disposal of Coy Commander	
		10.00	These will will be Platoon arrangements	
		11.00	Instruction in Drill Book	
		noon	Organized Games	
do	23/4/18	9.00	A.B.C. Coys at disposal of Company Commander CHD Coys ? T.T. under	
		10.00	Bde A.P.S. Lt.	
		11.15	Bombing Parade	
		14.00	A,B,C. Coys under Bn 4.G.S. Lt.G. & HD Coys at disposal of Coy Commander	
			Bombing ?	
			Two Drafts up to strength of 350 other ranks joined this Battalion	
do	24/4/18		Church Parade. The following service were held S.C.E. S of E at G.C. R.C.	
			Inspection of now draft by Commanding Officer.	
do	25/4/18	9.00	Coys at disposal Coy/Commander	
		10.00	Battalion Parade	

WAR DIARY
or
INTELLIGENCE SUMMARY.

Army Form C. 2118.

Place	Date	Hour	Summary of Events and Information	Remarks and references to Appendices
BONDUES	25/11/18	11.00 11.30 14.00	Physical Training. Lecture to Coy. Commanders. Subject "Road discipline applicable to present conditions". Company Drill - order - Close Order Drill. Platoon, Squad, & Arms drills now proceed to engage a rear officer & N.C.O's also Squad drill in the following expect experience - foot-drill with & without arms - Loading & Firing, Bayonet fighting.	
do	26/11/18	10.00 11.00	Brigade Commanders Parade. A/D.A.D.S. Capt. B. Stanford C attended and Company of guns. Area Cleaning teams	
do	27/11/18 10.00	11.00	At 10 Infantry Brigade Group was inspected by XI Corps Commander. Dispersing to Green's Reading Hall	
do	28/11/18	11.30 15.00	Horse Parade under Coy. arrangements. Lecture by Coy Commanders. Subject - Lieut-General Douglas. On road under allotted this task on the Francis 1st N.S.S.L., N.O.S.F. Lecture held in the Corps Pictures Hall General R.A.F. Training signed. Conversation between Police & Public.	
do	29/11/18	09.00 10.15 12.00 14.30	Commanding Officers Parade. Snooker Bayonet fighting & Toy Gloves. 42 Officers NCO's Cadets & ? did not attend entertainment given by Major D. Brown Jerome in the Copper Cinema Hall. Lecture Subject "Demobilisation"	

Army Form C. 2118.

WAR DIARY
or
INTELLIGENCE SUMMARY.

(Erase heading not required.)

Place	Date	Hour	Summary of Events and Information	Remarks and references to Appendices
BORDVES	30/11/18	10.00	B.G.C. Inspection of Battalions Billets Organized Games & Football &c.	11.37
		14.00		

Geo. Hoffman Major
O/C 18th York & Lancaster Rgt.

SECRET   Copy No. 14

OPERATION ORDERS No. 23
by Capt. G.W. JEFFERSON, Commanding,
18th Batt. York & Lancaster Regiment.

November 8th 1918.

1. MOVE
On the night of the 8th/9th Novr. the 13th Batt. York & Lancaster Regt. will be relieved by the 12th Batt. Suffolk Regt.
Relief will be complete by 00.01 Nov. 9th

2. RELIEF
Companies will be relieved in the following order -
A Coy York & Lancs Regt by A Coy Suffolk Regt.
B   "   do   by C "   do
C   "   do   by B "   do
D   "   do   by D "   do

3. GUIDES
Five guides per Coy, (one per platoon and one per Coy Headqrs) and two guides per Batt. Headqrs will report to Sgt. Dutton at 16.30 at Batt. Headqrs to be conducted to the rendezvous at Cross Roads at C 1 a 20.85

4. TRENCH STORES
All Defence schemes, aeroplane photos, maps, Trench Stores will be handed over to incoming unit and receipt in duplicate will be obtained and forwarded to Batt. Headqrs by 09.00 on 9th Nov.

5. BATTALION STORES
O.C. Coys will be responsible that all petrol tins cooking utensils etc., on their establishment are conveyed to their new billets.

6. ORDERS to O.C. T.M.B. Section will be issued later.

7. ROUTE
(a) On completion of relief Coys will march to their billets in new area 37/ A 22 a 87 by route BOIS JACQUET - DOTTIGNIES - QUEVAUCAMP - WATTRELOS and report their arrival and location to Batt. Headqrs.

(b) All movement EAST of a line ESTIMPUIS - CROMBION will be by platoons at 200 yards interval.

8. Lieut. T.V. Skidmore and one N.C.O. per Coy and Batt. Headqrs will report at 10.00 at B.H.Q. and proceed to new area to take over new billets at 37/ A 22 a 87 and will meet their respective Coys coming from the line at A 16 d 65.40

9. BILLETS
All billets will be handed over in a clean and tidy condition.

10. COMPLETION OF RELIEF
Relief complete will be reported by BAB Code.

Sheet No. 2

11. TRANSPORT LINES
(a) Transport will move to 37/ A 22 a 27 and can commence moving after 11.00 on 8th Novr.

(b) Transport of relieving units will commence arriving in present lines at 11.00 on 8th Novr.

(c) No extra transport will be available - all stores must be moved by Regimental transport.

12. Acknowledge:

8/11/18

J. J. Mundy, 2/Lieut. & A/Adjt.,
18th York & Lancaster Regt.

Copies to:
1. 41st Inf. Bde.
2. C.O.
3. Adjutant
4. O.C. A Coy
5. O.C. B Coy
6. O.C. C. Coy
7. O.C. D Coy
8. H.Q. Coy
9. M.O.
10. Q.M.
11. T.O.
12. O.C. T.M.B.
13. War Diary
14. War Diary
15. File
16. R.S.M.

SECRET

BATTALION ORDERS NO. 24
by Capt. G.W. JEFFERSON, Commanding.
18th York & Lancaster Regt.

Copy No 14.

Ref.Sheet 36. 1/40,000
Ref.Sheet 37. 1/40,000

13/11/18

1. MOVE

On the 14/11/18 the 41st Infantry Brigade Group will move from Herseaux-Wattrelos Area to the BONDUES Area.

(b) The 18th Bn. York & Lancs. Regt will move from WATTRELOS to BONDUES 36/E.23.b.69.

2. PARADES

(a) The Battalion will parade in the following order -
"A" Coy. "H.Q." "B" "C" "D" Coy and Transport.

(b) Lewis Gun limbers and Cookers to parade with their Companies.
(c) The head of the column will march off from the Square, WATTRELOS at 09.00.
(d) Companies and Transport will march at an interval of 100 yards.

3. DRESS

Fighting Order less haversack and great coat. Steel helmets to be carried on the back of pack, and jerkins will be carried in the pack. S.B.Rs. will be carried.

4. MARCH DISCIPLINE

March discipline will be rigourously carried out. All halts as previously laid down will be by the whistle. Coy and Platoon Officers will pay particular attention to the paying of compliments to General Officers, guards, etc.

5. STORES

(a) Sandbags, blankets, Signalling & Medical stores to be at Qr.Mr.Stores at 07.00.
(b) Officers valises and mess kits to be at Q.M.Stores by 08.00
(c) One G.S. wagon will report at "A" Coy H.Q. at 07.00 to clear sandbags, blankets, officers kits e
(d) Orderly Room boxes to be ready for loading at 06.00.

6. RATIONS.

Will be carried on Field Kitchen limbers.

7. COOKING.

Coys will arrange to make tea on the march to be served on arrival. Dinners will be served at 16.30.

8. BILLETS

Will be left in a clean and tidy condition. Certificate as per pro forma attached will be signed by all owners of billets and returned to B.O. Room by 06.30. All claims to be settled before leaving.

9. BILLETING PARTY.

2/Lieut. J.A. Askin and one N.C.O. per Coy will proceed from B.O. Room at 06.00 on cycles to meet Staff Captain at BONDUES Church at 09.30.

10. LORRIES.

(a) Two 3-ton lorries will be allotted to this Battalion.
(b) Lorries can make two journeys if required.
(c) additional lorries may be available.
(d) The Q.M. will detail two Other ranks to meet lorries at 06.50 at HERSEAUX to guide them to Q.M.Stores.

11. SUPPLIES

Supplies for the 14th inst will be delivered to Transport lines on completion of the march.
Transport Sergt. will immediately on arrival, send a mounted Orderly to No. 2 Coy. Train at F 1 c 11 to guide supply wagons to the Transport lines.

Sheet No. 2.

12. RETURNS
    (a) O.C.Coys, Q.M.Stores and Transport will immediately on arrival notify B.O.Room of the location of their H.Q. (map reference)

    (b) Coys will render within an hour of arrival a "Falling Out" state as follows:
        (a) Nos. who fell out and did not rejoin.
        (b) Nos. who fell out and rejoined on the march.
    Ref. (a) Cause of falling out.
    Ref. (b) Cause of falling out.
    stating time away from line of march.
    Every man falling out is to be in possession of a chit signed by an officer.
    (c) Will also render by 20.00 on 14th inst a return of all billets occupied by their Coys, etc, on the following pro-forma :

Coy.	Billet		Accommodation			Remarks.
	Name of Street	No. of Billet.	Officers.	Men.	Horses.	

To be stated in this column if available for Officers' Mess, N.C.Os. Mess, Offices, Aid Post, Q.M.Stores, etc.

ACKNOWLEDGE.

                                    J. Mundy.   Lieut. & A/Adjt.
Issued at   13th York & Lancs.Regt.
23.30.

Copies to :

1. C.O.   7. H.Q.
2. Adjutant.   8. Q.M.   13. 41st Inf.Bde.
3. O.C."A" Coy.   9. Transport.   14. War Diary.
4. O.C. "B" Coy.   10. O.C.41st T.M.B.   15. War Diary.
5. O.C."C" Coy.   11. M.O.   16. File.
6. O.C."D " Coy.   12. R.S.M.

C O N F I D E N T I A L.

W A R   D I A R Y

- of -

18th YORK & LANCASTER REGT.

From: 1st December, 1918.
To: 31st December, 1918.

VOLUME VII.

WAR DIARY
or
INTELLIGENCE SUMMARY.

(Erase heading not required.)

Army Form C. 2118.

Place	Date	Hour	Summary of Events and Information	Remarks and references to Appendices
BONDUES	1/2/18	0930 1000	Coy at disposal of Coy Commanders. Church Parade. C of E. 10.0 Rm C of S. 9.30 R.C. 6.	A II.
do	2/2/18	9.30 12.30	Coy at disposal of Coy Commanders. 4 Officers & Sgts attended C.O. to arrange Rubin Lectures at the "Cigne Grene" Grene Place Grene Street Company Education Classes in Spelling, Arithmetic & Letter writing continued. Education Parades.	A II
do	3/2/18	0920 1300 1000 1000 1120	No 1 Coy. R.E. & Games. No 2 Coy. Bathing & Drill Ceremonial do A Coy. Rifle Exercises. B Coy. do	A II
do	4/2/18	0915 1400	No 1 & 2 Coys. Working Party. A & B Coys. At disposal of Coy Commanders for Educational Classes & recreational arrangement.	A II
do	5/2/18	0930 1300	Coy at disposal of Coy Commanders. Parties were sent under the direction of the Battalion for Working parties, Continuation of the Cigne Grene Education Classes & recreation in the afternoon	A II

Army Form C. 2118.

WAR DIARY
or
INTELLIGENCE SUMMARY.
(Erase heading not required.)

Place	Date	Hour	Summary of Events and Information	Remarks and references to Appendices
BONDUES	6.12.18	9900 1400	Rehearsal for Army Commander's inspection. Organised Games. Being finals of divisional Boxing Competition held at TURCOING. Preliminary notice Lance Corporal Heavyweight Competition. The following Draft Reinforcements arrived. Drove to Estrée – Tambour – Major of the Crown Prince. Disputes The Governors.	
	7.12.18	9900 7.30	Physical training & Baths. Rifle exam, cleaning & equipment.	
	8.12.18	9700	Spring Drill squadrons by officers. Rifle exam of TURCOING.	
	9.12.18	9900 1.30	Guard duties. B.P.S. Hand Exam. Company orders. Physical training Games. Unit training programme 6. Claim of the Division at TURCOING.	
	10.12.18	9900	Horse, Ambulance, Bicycles, Motors. Battery, Ordnance riches, Commanding Officer's Parade. Drawing ordered, as ordered by the Corps Commander.	
	11.12.18	9900	Cleaning of equipment. Rehearsal of Training Kennels. Kits & Equipment inspection. Greatcoat marking. Educational classes as per programme. Commencement of refresher specialist courses.	
	12.12.18	9900	Physical training & games. Education. Reading & Pictures. Soccer series in the Cycle. Lecture at TURCOING by Rev. E. Howard Kennedy on Bolshevism.	

Army Form C. 2118.

WAR DIARY
or
INTELLIGENCE SUMMARY.
(Erase heading not required.)

Instructions regarding War Diaries and Intelligence Summaries are contained in F. S. Regs., Part II. and the Staff Manual respectively. Title pages will be prepared in manuscript.

Place	Date	Hour	Summary of Events and Information	Remarks and references to Appendices
BOMDVE9	13.12.18	0900	Physical Training Games & Chasing &c. Education. Debates & platoons. Games in Front. Kettle Keeping Lectures.	A.
	14.12.18		Commanding Officers made Inspection of Lines. Officials Ordering of Lines. Medical Inspection of Lines. Gathering appearance of General Oder for Drawing Blankets. Lecture at Theatre by Capt. Lerk, Navigator. "Captains in Life".	B.
	15.12.18		Church Services same as on Sunday 8th by C. of E & R.C.	C.
	16.12.18	0730	Physical Training Games. Education Reading & Writing. Church Parade. Service took Duty and followed Nature Hours. R. Coat Service at 1030.	D.
	17.12.18	0900	Physical Training Games. Education Writing by Dictation. Lecture by Educational Officer in Parliament. Awaiting Passenger Early Reserve Courses in Catch Sunday of P.R.I.	E.

D. D. & L., London, E.C.

Army Form C. 2118.

WAR DIARY
or
INTELLIGENCE SUMMARY.
(Erase heading not required.)

Place	Date	Hour	Summary of Events and Information	Remarks and references to Appendices
BOVES.	18.12.18	10.00	Parade. Company at disposal of Company Commanders.	
		09.00	Education. Mental arithmetic by Platoons.	
			Nom. roll returned to Bde. Rfts. not being of use to Bn. personnel in Germany. Copies were sent to and the following all ranks to "Pretine i.c. TORBONE.	
	19.12.18	09.00	Battalion letter.	
			Education. Geography by Platoons.	
			Interested Recreational nature.	
	20.12.18	10.00	Cheveaux country walk. Physical training & Games.	
		09.00	Letter by Platoons. Impact hand writing.	
			Cheveaux pronounce to make up Kalmar.	
		10.00	Court Polaky assembled to investigate Complaint illegal posting of assistance of Pte (Ranty?) 5373 & the PLUTOT Pte Signal Sheicswell between Pte Kellis of 2006 and 2050.	
	21.12.18	11.00	Commanding Officers' Parade.	
		09.00	Debate of Sharemen Subject Demobilization & Recruitment on	
	22.12.18		Church Parade.	
			Lecture at MOUVEAUX by Col E L Ham C.M.G services were held. Stated the new English Rivalries to Germany what effect, the new English Rivalries military from the victory of the Empire	

Army Form C. 2118.

WAR DIARY
or
INTELLIGENCE SUMMARY.
(Erase heading not required.)

Instructions regarding War Diaries and Intelligence Summaries are contained in F. S. Regs., Part II. and the Staff Manual respectively. Title pages will be prepared in manuscript.

Place	Date	Hour	Summary of Events and Information	Remarks and references to Appendices
BORDUES	23.12.18	10.00	Parades under Coy arrangements	
			Education. Reading by officers.	
			Church Service. Housekeeping duties	
	26.12.18	8.30 9.30 7.30	Company Inspection	M.A.
			Rifle training games	
			Field Coy arrangements	
		10.30	Education. Distinguisher station arrangements	A
	25.12.18		Church Parade. C of E. Am. R.C. & P & Services.	M.A.
	26.12.18	9.00 1/30	Company Games & Sports	
			Platoon event	
	27.12.18	9.00 9.30 11.00 12.00 14.00	Inspection	
			Rifle Parade & Lectures	
			Lecture on Gas & Chemistry	
			Training	
			Inter platoon sports competitions	
	28.12.18	9.00 1.00 9.30	Company Inspection	A.A.
			Platoon Drill	
			Company meals in Emergency after Coy pair...	
			Left 7 station recruits remaining R.Q.S. Gas see keys	
			L/C Jefferson proceed on leave to U.K.	

WAR DIARY
or
INTELLIGENCE SUMMARY.

(Erase heading not required.)

Army Form C. 2118.

Place	Date	Hour	Summary of Events and Information	Remarks and references to Appendices
BOUAVES	29.12.17		Church Parade. O.P.C. Service. C.O.L.R.C.	
	30.12.17	9 am	Inspection of approach of Equipment. Interior Economy, exterior in English, bathing parties headed by Band & Drum. All ranks Ettournes Kanotteers & Advanced Registration. Regimental Games, Interplatoon football.	
	31.12.17	9 am 9.30	Battalion Inspection. Column of 261 m.t.m. musordigal football.	

Claurs Vinno Capt
Comdg. 18th Bn. York & Lancaster Regt.

Original 14

Army Form C. 2118.

WAR DIARY
and
INTELLIGENCE SUMMARY.
(Erase heading not required.)

Confidential

War Diary
of
18th York and Lancaster Regt

Volume 8.

From 1/1/19.
To 31/1/19.

Army Form C. 2118.

WAR DIARY
or
INTELLIGENCE SUMMARY.
(Erase heading not required.)

Place	Date	Hour	Summary of Events and Information	Remarks and references to Appendices
BONDUES	1.1.19	0900	Parades, Inspection & Arms Drill. P.T. & Games. Education Classes in French, Bookkeeping, Shorthand. French, Elementary Education - Mental Arithmetic, Dictation etc. Capt. Lt. Laver Irvine assumed command of the Batt: vice Major J. Harden. Vice Major Ed. Jefferson.	Appx.
do.	2.1.19	0900 0930 1100	Infantry Training Platoon Education. Geography by Platoons. Lecture on History by Lt. Col. Burley.	Appx.
do.	3.1.19	0900 1400	Companies at disposal of O.C. Coy. Commander for the cleaning of billets. Inter-Platoon Football Competition. Regimental cinema & pictures in evening.	Appx.
do.	4.1.19	0900 1100	The Battalion moved to TOURCOING. Order No. 22 of 3.1.19. attached. Move complete.	Appendix 1.
TOURCOING	5.1.19		Church Parades. The following Church Parades were held. C. of E., Rom. Cath. & P. C.	Appx.

Army Form C. 2118.

WAR DIARY
or
INTELLIGENCE SUMMARY.
(Erase heading not required.)

Instructions regarding War Diaries and Intelligence Summaries are contained in F. S. Regs., Part II. and the Staff Manual respectively. Title pages will be prepared in manuscript.

Place	Date	Hour	Summary of Events and Information	Remarks and references to Appendices
TOURCOING	6.1.19	0900	Inspection & Arms Drill	nil
		1030	Physical Training & Games	
		1130	Musketry Lecture Various Educational. Reading under platoon arrangements classes in Field. Bookkeeping & Spelling	
do	7.1.19	0900	Inspection & Arms Drill	nil
		1030	Physical Training & Games.	
			Education. Outing under platoon arrangements.	
			2 Officers & 25 other ranks attended a Lecture on "War Aims"	
			6 Other ranks of Bn proceeded on Education Leave.	
			On Bn Board assembled to make records of Regt funds etc.	
do	8.1.19	0900	Inspection	nil
		1030	Tribe Alarm Lecture.	
		1100	P.T. & Games.	
		1400	Education. Writing under platoon arrangements	
do	9.1.19	0900	Inspection	nil
		0930	Physical Training & Games	
		1000	Education. Geography by platoons	
			Lecture on History by Rev. R.S. Bailey	

WAR DIARY
or
INTELLIGENCE SUMMARY.

(Erase heading not required.)

Army Form C. 2118.

Place	Date	Hour	Summary of Events and Information	Remarks and references to Appendices
TOURCOING	10.1.19	0900	Inspection	
		0930	Physical Training & Games	
		1100	Education. Gaiety, under, by arrangement, lecture: General Knowledge	
		1415	Lecture by the Chaplain, Chaplain. Discovery.	
			30 cadets attested to the Battalion	A.
		1300	First party of 200 men visited Lille & the pantomime	
do.	11.1.19	0900	Inspection	
		0930	Physical Training & Games.	
		1100	Company Drill	
		1115	Education. Company Debates: Town & Country Life	
		1400	Second party of 200 men visited Lille	
			Church Parade. The following transfers were held.	A.
do.	12.1.19		E.O. Pte Ln Cpt L.P. to Cpl Lord Pte Wild in Gunn Mess, Tourbere represented this Battalion.	
			Cpl Ed Hammond appointed to the Educational Officer Award. Le Belgian Croix de Guerre has been awarded to 309659 Sjt. Wood A Deset, "D" Coy 18th York & Lancs.	A.

Army Form C. 2118.

WAR DIARY
or
INTELLIGENCE SUMMARY.
(Erase heading not required.)

Instructions regarding War Diaries and Intelligence Summaries are contained in F. S. Regs., Part II. and the Staff Manual respectively. Title pages will be prepared in manuscript.

Place	Date	Hour	Summary of Events and Information	Remarks and references to Appendices
TOURCOING	13.1.19	0730	Inspection & Arms Drill Muskety	nil
		1000	Physical Training & Games	
			Education.	
			Reading by Platoons	
			In selecting classes men take French, English	
			Dutch & Chinese.	
do	14.1.19	0730	Inspection & Arms Drill	nil
		0930	Pay to men by Companies	
		1145	Physical Training & Games	
		1745	Education. Kupt individuals by platoons	
			Classes were held for Australia Bookkeeping	
		1600	Baths taken	
do	15.1.19	0730	Inspection & Arms Drill	nil
		0930	Physical Training & Games	
		1030	Education. Weekly exam given arranged	
			Received by G.O.C. at Hotel de Signe	
			Chaces were held in the following subjects French	
			Spelling Dictation & Dutch	
do	16.1.19	0730	Inspection & Arms Drill	nil
		0920	Physical Training Games	
		1030	Education. Exams by Platoons	
		1530	Classes were held in the following subjects French	
			Reading Spelling Bookkeeping	

Army Form C. 2118.

WAR DIARY
or
INTELLIGENCE SUMMARY.
(Erase heading not required.)

Instructions regarding War Diaries and Intelligence Summaries are contained in F. S. Regs., Part II. and the Staff Manual respectively. Title pages will be prepared in manuscript.

Place	Date	Hour	Summary of Events and Information	Remarks and references to Appendices
TOURCOING	17.11.19	0900	Inspection & Arms Drill	
		0930	Rifle drill. Gun drill under Education. Elementary French by platoons.	
		0930	Officers Lecture held by the following subject. Infantry & Music.	
			Arrivals. 2/Capt. R.S. Pickering 18 Lyrs & leave. No warrant for Military Ques.	
do	18.11.19	0900	Inspection & Arms Drill	
		0920	Physical Training & Games	
		1030	Education. Lecture by Capt R.S. Bailey to Infantry Sectors. Debate by Companies, subject "Beyond the Influence to 1st year and page the natural time than the Cavalry arm?" Cap A. Ling. C.S.E. act.	
do	19.11.19		The following Church Services were held.	
			R.C. — Lieut. Col. J. McLennan Emigne incenue arrival Field westered.	
			Mes. Capt E.C. Ferris Vicar.	
do	20.11.19	0900	Inspection & Arms Drill	
		0930	Rifle Inspection	
			Education. The following classes were held. French & Italian & Lecture and film in Cinema Hall Tourcoing by R.J. Baker. Subject. Gulls Atlantis & Yugoslavs. 30 seats allotted to the Battalion.	

Army Form C. 2118.

WAR DIARY
or
INTELLIGENCE SUMMARY.
(Erase heading not required.)

Instructions regarding War Diaries and Intelligence Summaries are contained in F. S. Regs., Part II. and the Staff Manual respectively. Title pages will be prepared in manuscript.

Place	Date	Hour	Summary of Events and Information	Remarks and references to Appendices
TOURGOINE	21/1/19	0900	Inspection C.A.S.B. Coys by Commanding Officer	
		1100	Physical Training Classes.	
			Education. Dictation by platoons.	
		0900	Classes were held at the following subjects. French, Bookkeeping, Spelling, Arithmetic.	
do	22/1/19	0900	Inspection of C.S.D. Coys by Commanding Officer.	
		1100	Physical Training Classes.	
		0900	Education. Sing Reading Dictation. Classes were held in the following subjects. French Education. HQ trench as appointed of Quartermaster was Bde orderly.	
do	23/1/19	0900	Inspection C Coy Drill	
		0930	Physical Training Classes.	
		1030	Education. Recital Dictation by platoons. Lecture by Capt E.H. Coleman Subject American History.	
do	24/1/19	0900	Inspection C Coy Drill	
		0930	Physical Training Classes.	
		1130	Musketry by platoons. General Education Dictation, Education. Subject General Knowledge. Classes were held in the following subjects. French, Arithmetic.	

D. D. & L., London, E.C.

WAR DIARY
or
INTELLIGENCE SUMMARY.
(Erase heading not required.)

Army Form C. 2118.

Instructions regarding War Diaries and Intelligence Summaries are contained in F. S. Regs., Part II. and the Staff Manual respectively. Title pages will be prepared in manuscript.

Place	Date	Hour	Summary of Events and Information	Remarks and references to Appendices
TOURCOING	25.1.19	0930	Battalion Parade. The Battalion marched to ROUBAIX to witness the presentation of colours to this Battalion by Lieut. General Sir Beauvoir De Lisle K.C.B. D.S.O. Commanding XV Corps. Awards: Military Service Medal awarded to 23005 Sgt. Beaumont G. 10th York & Lancs.	M.S.
do.	26.1.19		The following Church Services were held. Capt. T. Rev. Capt. R.T.C.	M.S.
do.	27.1.19	0900, 1020, 1130.	Inspections & Arms Drill Physical Training & Games Musketry Education. Platoon Education: General Knowledge Paper. Classes were held on the following subjects: French Arithmetic.	M.S.
do.	28.1.19	0900, 1030. 1130. 0930	Inspections & Arms Drill. Physical Training & Games. Musketry. Bolt Drill. Education Classes were held in the following subjects. Bookkeeping, Spelling, Dictation, & Arithmetic.	M.S.
do.	29.1.19	0900 0930	Inspections & Arms Drill. Companies at the discretion of Coy. Commanders. Education classes were held in the following subjects: Shorthand French.	M.S.

Army Form C. 2118.

WAR DIARY
or
INTELLIGENCE SUMMARY.
(Erase heading not required.)

Place	Date	Hour	Summary of Events and Information	Remarks and references to Appendices
TOURCOING	30.1.19	0900	Inspection & Route march.	
		1000	Physical Training Planned	
		11.00	Education. Lecture by Capt. F.W. Goodman, Subject American History. Classes were held on the following subject: Bookkeeping.	
do	31.1.19	0900	Inspection & Marching Exercise	
		1100	Lecture to the Batt. by B.S.E.	
		1000	Geography by Platoons. Classes were held on the following subjects: French & Shorthand.	

D. Mercer Lt. Col.
O/c 10th York Lancaster Rgt.

SECRET   18th YORK & LANCASTER REGIMENT   3-1-19

ORDER NO.... 22

Ref: Sheet 36 - 1/40,000

1. The 41st Infantry Brigade will move on January 3rd and 4th 1919 from the BONDUES area to the TOURCOING area and take over billets of the 43rd Infantry Brigade.

2. The 18th Battalion York & Lancaster Regt will move on January 4th 1919 and take over billets occupied by the 12th Bn.Suffolk Regt.

  (a) Companies and Transport will parade independently and move up to the starting points at E.1? 0.25 by 09.45, in the following order - Band, Headquarters. B.A.C.D.Coys and Transport.
  (b) Battalion will pass starting point at 10.00.
  (c) All movement will be by Companies at 100 yards interval. Twenty-five yards interval between each group of six vehicles.
  (d) Dress - FULL MARCHING ORDER. Soft caps will be worn.
  (e) Marching out state to be rendered to Adjutant at Starting Point.

4. Route -   Road Junction E.18.c.40.25
               Road Junction E.18.b.7.7.
               X Roads E.7.d.4.7.
               X Roads E.14.a.5.8.
               Thence to billets.

5. Arrival in Billets will be immediately reported to Battalion H.Q.

6. Personnel of 41st Inf. Bde. Agric. Coy. will return to their units Coys. at TOURCOING on the completion of the move.

ADMINISTRATIVE INSTRUCTIONS

1. Lorries.
Three lorries are allotted to the Battalion and will report at the Church, BONDUES at 08.00. The Quartermaster will detail a guide to direct lorries to their various duties.
Lorries will be allotted as follows:
         A & B Coys.....1 lorry.
         C & D " .....1 lorry.
         H.Q.Coy, Sgts.Mess & O.R.....1 lorry.

2. Blankets, Stores, Kits, etc.
  a) Each Company will form a dump at Coy. H.Q., of blankets tightly rolled in bundles of ten, Officers Kits and Stores. All dumps to be completed by 07.30 and left in charge of a guard of 1 N.C.O. and 3 men who will form the loading and unloading party, and will be responsible for the proper distribution of the stores on arrival at the new billets.
     Motor lorries report to Companies at 08.00.

(b) H.Q.Coy. will make similar arrangements. The lorry at their disposal will call first at Sergeant's Mess and then to Coy.Dump. In addition to the guard of 1 N.C.O and 3 men, the Sergts. Mess will arrange for 1 N.C.O. and 1 man to travel by this lorry.
Orderly Room and Canteen Stores will be picked up by the lorry on second journey.

NOTE: ANY STORES NOT CLEARED BY FIRST LOAD WILL BE DUMPED AT QUARTERMASTER'S STORES.

(d) Officers Mess kit will be packed and ready by 08.30. Officers of Battalion H.Q. will dump their kits at the H.Mess by 08.30

Sheet No. 2.

3. Billets.
(a) All billets to be left in a clean and sanitary condition.
(b) A certificate de Bien Vivre will be obtained from the proprietor of billets and returned to Battalion Orderly Room by 09.00
(c) All claims for damage &c., to be settled before leaving the area. If necessary, an officer of the Coy. concerned will be left behind to make a settlement.

4. Area Stores, etc.
(a) The following Stores will be handed over to the 12th Bn. Suffolk Regt.-

Beds.	Washbowls.	Forms
Paillasses	Latrines	Tables.
Ablution Benches.	Latrine Buckets.	Fire Buckets.

(b) All component parts of an Huts and Nissen Huts issued to units will be handed over.
(c) Receipts for all stores etc. handed over under Paras (a) & (b) above are to be obtained in duplicate by O.C.Coys, Q.M. and Transport Officer, and returned to Orderly Room immediately on completion of relief. A third copy will be given to incoming unit.
(d) Stores in the Recreation Room will be handed over by O.C."D" Coy.
(e) One Officer and one N.C.O per Coy will remain behind to hand over.

5. Rear Party
Sanitary men will remain behind for the purpose of clearing the billets of all refuse, and will report at the conclusion of their duties to Officers handing over billets, at Batt. H.Q. and will march to new billets under senior officer.

6. Fire Orders.
In view of the nature of buildings occupied as billets in the TOURCOING area, special attention is to be paid to ensuring that all fire orders are complied with.
Copies of Fire Orders for the Brigade Area in TOURCOING are attached (Appendix "A"). These will be posted in prominent places in Company billets.

7. Medical
Sick in TOURCOING are evacuated by 44th Field Ambulance.

J. Mundy.
Captain,
A/Adjutant,
18th York & Lancs. Regt.

Issued to :-

Bde. H.Q.,
2. C.O,
3. Adjt.
4. O.C. "A" Coy.
5. O.C. "B" Coy.
6. O.C. "C" Coy.
7. O.C. "D" Coy.
8. O.C. "H.Q." Coy.
9 H.Q.
10 Q.M.
11 T.O.
12 R.S.M.
13 War Diary.
14 War Diary.
15 File.
16 File.

WAR DIARY

~~INTELLIGENCE SUMMARY~~
(Erase heading not required.)

Army Form C. 2118.

Confidential
War Diary
of
18th York and Lancaster Regt.

From 1/2/19.
To 28/2/19.
Volume 9.

WAR DIARY
or
INTELLIGENCE SUMMARY

Army Form C. 2118.

Place	Date	Hour	Summary of Events and Information	Remarks and references to Appendices
TOURCOING	1.2.19	0930 / 1100 / 1000	Inspection & Marching Exercise. Physical Training & Games. Platoon Education. Reading & writing useful literature. Classes were held.	
do.	2.2.19		The following Church Services were held & g.c. T.C. Arm C.F.S.	
do.	3.2.19	0930 / 1100 / 1000	Inspection & Marching Exercise. Physical Training & Games. Platoon Education. Geography. Classes were held in the following subjects: Shorthand & French	
do.	4.2.19	0930 / 1000 / 1100	Inspection & Marching Exercise. Physical Training & Games. Platoon Education. Reading by platoons. Shorthand classes were held. Battalion football match. Musical Ratts.	
do.	5.2.19	0700 / 1000 / 1000 / 1100	Physical Training & Games. Lecture by Capt. all Stockman.	
do.	6.2.19	0930 / 1000 / 1600	Inspection & Marching Exercise. Physical Training & Games. Platoon Education. Reading by Platoons. Bookkeeping classes were held. A lecture by W. Wilkins was given in the C.H.R.O.E. Hutz by Lt. B.A.K. Urgent Settings and Geography. 20 were to attend to the Lecture.	

Army Form C. 2118.

WAR DIARY
or
INTELLIGENCE SUMMARY.
(Erase heading not required.)

Instructions regarding War Diaries and Intelligence Summaries are contained in F. S. Regs., Part II. and the Staff Manual respectively. Title pages will be prepared in manuscript.

Place	Date	Hour	Summary of Events and Information	Remarks and references to Appendices
TOURCOING	7.2.19	09.00	Inspection & Musketry Exercises	Staff
		10.00	Physical Training & Games	
		11.00	Education. Working of Regl. Platoon	
		16.00	Class held in French & Shorthand. A lecture was given by No 2nd B[attalio]n of the Engrs Electric ROUBAIX	
			Subject "German Aims & Intentions."	
	8.2.19	09.00	Inspection Musketry & Exercise	Staff
		10.00	Physical Training & Games	Staff
		11.00	Education. General Knowledge by Platoons	Staff
	9.2.19	11.45	Commanding Officers Church Parade.	Staff
	10.2.19	09.00	Inspection & Arms Drill.	
		10.00	Physical Training & Games	
		11.00	Education. Arithmetic by Platoons	Staff
		13.00		
		15.00	Battalion Bathing at 4th Div Baths	Staff
"	11.2.19	09.00	Inspection & Musketry Exercises	
		10.00	Physical Training & Games	
		11.00	Education. English Grammar by Platoon	
	12.2.19	09.00	Inspection & Musketry Exercise	Staff
		10.00	Physical Training & Games	
		11.00	Lecture by 2nd Lt W.S.P Mason on "Parliament"	
	13.2.19	09.00	Inspection & Musketry Exercise	Staff
		10.00	Physical Training & Games.	
		11.00	Education. Reading & Very Exp[ensive]	

Army Form C. 2118.

WAR DIARY
or
INTELLIGENCE SUMMARY.
(Erase heading not required.)

Instructions regarding War Diaries and Intelligence Summaries are contained in F.S. Regs., Part II. and the Staff Manual respectively. Title pages will be prepared in manuscript.

Place	Date	Hour	Summary of Events and Information	Remarks and references to Appendices
TOURRAIN G.	13-2-19	09.00	Inspection + Marching Exercise	Ref.
		10.00	Physical Training + Games	
		11.00	Education. Reading. Reg. Bog	
			Owing to the smallness of boys on A. I. investigation arrangements were made for transfers of the Battalion in for 6 to companies	Ref.
	14-2-19	09.00	Inspection + Marching Exercise	
		10.00	Physical Training + Games	
		11.00	Education. Writing	
	15-2-19		Classes were held in French + Shorthand	Ref.
		09.00	Inspection + Marching. Exercise	
		09.30	Physical Training + Games	Ref.
		10.30	Education — General Knowledge	
	16-2-19	11.00	Commanding Officers Church Parade	Ref.
		11.45	Holy Communion	
	17-2-19	09.00	Inspection. Rioting. Classes were held in French + Shorthand	Ref.
		09.30	Education	
	18-2-19	09.00	Inspection.	
		09.30	Education. "English Grammar."	Ref.
	19-2-19	09.00	Adjs. tactical Parade of Inspection	
		09.30	Education. Geography. Classes were held in French + Shorthand	Ref.
			Owing to Demobilisation arrangements were made to form a composite Company of the men left in the Battalion	

WAR DIARY
or
INTELLIGENCE SUMMARY.

(Erase heading not required.)

Army Form C. 2118.

Place	Date	Hour	Summary of Events and Information	Remarks and references to Appendices
TOURCOING	20.2.19	09.00	Adjutants Parade & Inspection	Nil
		09.30	Physical Training & Games	
		10.30	Education. Reading.	
	21.2.19	09.00	Commanding Officers Parade & Inspection. The Commanding Officer lectured the Battalion on the Advantages of Re-enlisting in the Post Bellum Army.	Nil
		10.00	Physical Training & Games.	
		11.00	Lecture. English History. Rev. R.E.S. Bailey	
"	22.2.19	09.00	Adjutants Parade	Nil
		09.30	Physical Training & Games	
		10.30	Education. General Knowledge.	
"	23.2.19	11.00	Commanding Officers Church Parade	Nil
		11.45	Holy Communion.	
"	24.2.19	09.00	Adjutants Parade	Nil
		09.30	Education. Reading.	
		10.30	Physical Training & Games.	
"	25.2.19	09.00	Adjutants Parade	Nil
		09.30	Education. Grammar	
		10.30	Physical Training & Games.	

Army Form C. 2118.

WAR DIARY
or
INTELLIGENCE SUMMARY.
(Erase heading not required.)

Instructions regarding War Diaries and Intelligence Summaries are contained in F.S. Regs., Part II. and the Staff Manual respectively. Title pages will be prepared in manuscript.

Place	Date	Hour	Summary of Events and Information	Remarks and references to Appendices
TOURCOING	26/7/19	09.00	Adjutants Parade	Appx
		09.30	Education Geography	Appx
		10.30	Physical Training + Games	
	27/7/19	09.00	Adjutants Parade	Appx
		09.30	Education Arithmetic	
		10.30	Physical Training + Games	
"	28/7/19	09.00	Adjutants Parade	
			Education Reading	
			Physical Training + Games	

McClure, Lt Col
Commdg 10th Batt. K.O. (R. Lancaster Regt)

Original

Army Form C. 2118.

Instructions regarding War Diaries and Intelligence Summaries are contained in F.S. Regs., Part II. and the Staff Manual respectively. Title pages will be prepared in manuscript.

WAR DIARY

~~INTELLIGENCE SUMMARY~~

(Erase heading not required.)

Hour, Date, Place	Summary of Events and Information	Remarks and references to Appendices

Confidential

War Diary

of

18th York and Lancaster Regt.

From 1/3/19.   To 31/3/19.

Volume 10.

WAR DIARY
INTELLIGENCE SUMMARY

Army Form C. 2118.

Place	Date	Hour	Summary of Events and Information	Remarks and references to Appendices
Touraing	1/3/19	0900	Battalion Parade	
		0930	Education. General knowledge under Coy arrangements	
		1030	Physical Training Resumed	
do	2/3/19	1100	C of E Church Service. Summer Time commenced at 23.00. Time put forward one hour.	
do	3/3/19	0900	Adjutants Parade. 2nd Lieut James transferred to TOURCOING Area Clearing Coy 6.	
do	4/3/19	0900	Adjutants Parade. Owing to reduced numbers of Battalion through demobilisation, Education & training parades are suspended, all other ranks being employed at working parties &c.	
do	5/3/19	0900	Adjutants Parade, working parties &c.	
do	6/3/19	0900	Adjutants Parade, working parties &c.	
do	7/3/19	0900	Battalion Visited at Municipal Baths, working parties &c.	
do	8/3/19	0900	Working parties for removal of Area Stores etc	
do	9/3/19	1100	C of E Service in Church Army.	
		11.30	Commanding Officer inspected Battalion billets.	

Army Form C. 2118.

WAR DIARY
or
INTELLIGENCE SUMMARY.
(Erase heading not required.)

Instructions regarding War Diaries and Intelligence Summaries are contained in F. S. Regs., Part II and the Staff Manual respectively. Title pages will be prepared in manuscript.

Place	Date	Hour	Summary of Events and Information	Remarks and references to Appendices
Salisbury	10/3/19		Battalion moved to new billets at Factory, Rue de la Gare, Tourcoing.	Ref.
do	11/3/19	0900	The Battalion on parade purposes of instructions will parade as one Coy. Coy parade. Working parties.	Ref.
do	12/3/19	0900	Company parade. Working parties etc.	Ref.
do	13/3/19	0900	Company parade. Working parties.	Ref.
do	14/3/19	0900	Company parade. Working party.	Ref.
do	15/3/19	0900	Company parade. Working party.	Ref.
do	16/3/19	—	Church Parades in Church Army Chapel.	Ref.
do	17/3/19	1030	Inspection of billets by G.O.C.	Ref.
do	18/3/19	0900	Company Parade. Working Party.	Ref.
do	19/3/19	0900	Company Parade. Working Parade.	Ref.

Army Form C. 2118.

WAR DIARY
or
INTELLIGENCE SUMMARY.
(Erase heading not required.)

Instructions regarding War Diaries and Intelligence Summaries are contained in F.S. Regs., Part II. and the Staff Manual respectively. Title pages will be prepared in manuscript.

Place	Date	Hour	Summary of Events and Information	Remarks and references to Appendices
Inversing	21/3/19	0900	Company Parade. Working Parties.	Nil
do	21/3/19	0900	Company Parade. Working Parties.	Nil
do	22/3/19	0900	Company Parade. Working Parties.	Nil
do	23/3/19	—	Church Services in Church Army Chapel	Nil
do	24/3/19	0900	Boxing at Boulieu.	Nil
do	25/3/19	0900	Company Parade	Nil
do	26/3/19	0900	Company Parade. Wat. Pol. Lectures	Nil
do	27/3/19	—	Battalion moved to new Billets at Place Notre Dame, Toulouse	Nil
do	28/3/19	0900	Company Parade	Nil
do			Promulgated J.S.C.M. on 5379 Pte F. Bourke	Nil
do	29/3/19	0900	Company Parade.	Nil
do	30/3/19	0900	Company Parade	Nil
do	31/3/19	0900	Company Parade	Nil

M. Mari. Maj. 16/66
Cdg 18th York Lancaster Regt.

Original

Army Form C. 2118.

WAR DIARY
~~INTELLIGENCE SUMMARY~~
(Erase heading not required.)

Instructions regarding War Diaries and Intelligence Summaries are contained in F.S. Regs., Part II. and the Staff Manual respectively. Title pages will be prepared in manuscript.

Hour, Date, Place	Summary of Events and Information	Remarks and references to Appendices

Confidential
War Diary
of
18th York and Lancaster Regt.

From 1/4/1919.   To 30/4/1919.

Volume 11.

Army Form C. 2118.

WAR DIARY
or
INTELLIGENCE SUMMARY.
(Erase heading not required.)

Hour, Date, Place	Summary of Events and Information	Remarks and references to Appendices
TOURCOING 1/4/19	09.00 - 09.30 Inspection of Arms & kit. 09.30 - 10.30 P.T & Games. 10.30 - 12.00 at disposal of O/C Coy.	Muff
" 2/4/19	As for 1st/4/19.	Muff
" 3/4/19	As for 1st/4/19.	Muff
" 4/4/19	Battalion Bathing.	Muff
" 5/4/19	As for 1/4/19.	Muff
" 6/4/19	Church Parade at 11.00 at Church Army Chapel.	Muff
" 7/4/19	As for 1/4/19.	Muff
" 8/4/19	3 Officers & 80 O.R. demobilisable personnel under A.O. for Army of Occupation were posted to No 128 P.O.W. Coy	Muff
" 9/4/19	3. 6 Officers & 80 O.R. demobilisable personnel under A.O. 55.9.19.19 for Army of Occupation were posted to No 137 P.O.W Coy	Muff
" 10/4/19	09.00 Inspection (NOTE) Owing to demobilisation & despatch of above drafts on 8/4/19 & 9/4/19 sufficient personnel only was left to carry on the unit. From this date duties or class have not been resumed	Muff

Army Form C. 2118.

WAR DIARY
or
INTELLIGENCE SUMMARY.
(*Erase heading not required.*)

Instructions regarding War Diaries and Intelligence Summaries are contained in F. S. Regs., Part II. and the Staff Manual respectively. Title pages will be prepared in manuscript.

Hour, Date, Place		Summary of Events and Information	Remarks and references to Appendices
TOURCOING	11/4/19	Preparation 09.00 hrs	[illegible]
"	12/4/19	"	[illegible]
"	13/4/19	"	[illegible]
"	14/4/19	"	[illegible]
"	15/4/19	"	[illegible]
"	16/4/19	"	[illegible]
"	17/4/19	"	[illegible]
"	18/4/19	"	[illegible]
"	19/4/19	"	[illegible]
"	20/4/19	"	[illegible]
"	21/4/19	"	[illegible]
"	22/4/19	"	[illegible]
"	23/4/19	"	[illegible]
"	24/4/19	"	[illegible]
"	25/4/19	"	[illegible]
"	26/4/19	"	[illegible]
"	27/4/19	"	[illegible]
"	28/4/19	"	[illegible]
"	29/4/19	"	[illegible]
"	30/4/19	"	[illegible]

McPherson, Lieut. Col.
18th York & Lancs.

Original

Army Form C. 2118.

182/16

WAR DIARY

~~INTELLIGENCE SUMMARY.~~

(Erase heading not required.)

Instructions regarding War Diaries and Intelligence Summaries are contained in F. S. Regs., Part II. and the Staff Manual respectively. Title pages will be prepared in manuscript.

Hour, Date, Place	Summary of Events and Information	Remarks and references to Appendices

Confidential
War Diary
of
18th York and Lancaster Regt.

From 1/5/1919.　　　To 31/5/1919.

Volume 12.

(9 29 6) W 4141—463 100,000 9/14 H W V   Forms/C. 2118/10

Army Form C. 2118.

WAR DIARY
or
INTELLIGENCE SUMMARY.

(Erase heading not required.)

Instructions regarding War Diaries and Intelligence Summaries are contained in F. S. Regs., Part II. and the Staff Manual respectively. Title pages will be prepared in manuscript.

Place	Date	Hour	Summary of Events and Information	Remarks and references to Appendices
TOURCOING	1.5.19	09.00	Inspection. Battalion now reduced to Cadre establishment of 7 Off 46 OR	[sig]
"	2.5.19	09.00	Inspection	[sig]
"	3.5.19	09.00	"	[sig]
"	4.5.19	09.00	"	[sig]
"	5.5.19	09.00	"	[sig]
"	6.6.19	09.00	"	[sig]
"	7.5.19	09.00	"	[sig]
"	8.5.19	09.00	"	[sig]
"	9.5.19	09.00	"	[sig]
"	10.5.19	09.00	"	[sig]
"	11.5.19	09.00	"	[sig]
"	12.5.19	09.00	"	[sig]
"	13.5.19	09.00	"	[sig]
"	14.5.19	09.00	"	[sig]
"	15.5.19	09.00	"	[sig]
"	16.5.19	09.00	"	[sig]
"	17.5.19	09.00	"	[sig]
"	18.5.19	09.00	"	[sig]
"	19.5.19	09.00	"	[sig]
"	19.5.19	09.00	Cadre now reduced to establishment of 3 Off. 36 OR.	[sig]
"	20.5.19	09.00	"	[sig]
"	21.5.19	09.00	"	[sig]
"	22.5.19	09.00	"	[sig]

Army Form C. 2118.

WAR DIARY
or
INTELLIGENCE SUMMARY.
(Erase heading not required.)

Instructions regarding War Diaries and Intelligence Summaries are contained in F. S. Regs, Part II. and the Staff Manual respectively. Title pages will be prepared in manuscript.

Place	Date	Hour	Summary of Events and Information	Remarks and references to Appendices
TOURCOING	23.5.19	09.00	Inspection	
"	24.5.19	09.00	"	
"	25.5.19	09.00	"	
"	26.5.19	09.00	"	
"	27.5.19	09.00	"	
"	28.5.19	09.00	"	
"	29.5.19	09.00	"	
"	30.5.19	09.00	"	
"	31.5.19	09.00	"	

McLaren
LT. COLONEL
COMMANDING 1st BN. SCOTS GUARDS REGT.

www.ingramcontent.com/pod-product-compliance
Lightning Source LLC
Chambersburg PA
CBHW081432160426
43193CB00013B/2256